F.So.

How

TO SUCCEED

IN BUSINESS

WITHOUT

A PENIS

Also by

KAREN SALMANSOHN

HOW TO MAKE YOUR MAN BEHAVE IN 21 DAYS
OR LESS, USING THE SECRETS OF PROFESSIONAL
DOG TRAINERS

50% OFF, A NOVEL

How
TO SUCCEED
IN BUSINESS
WITHOUT
A PENIS

SECRETS AND
STRATEGIES
for the
WORKING
WOMAN

by

KAREN SALMANSOHN

HARMONY BOOKS / NEW YORK

Grateful acknowledgment is given for use of the following: © Copyright 1993 Portia Nelson from *There's a Hole in My Sidewalk,* Beyond Words Publishing, Hillsboro, Oregon. From THE POETRY OF ROBERT FROST edited by Edward Connery Lathem. Copyright 1942 by Robert Frost, © 1969 by Henry Holt and Co., Inc. © 1970 by Leslie Frost Ballantine. Reprinted by permission of Henry Holt and Co., Inc.

Published by Harmony Books, a division of Crown Publishers, Inc., 201 East 50th Street, New York, New York 10022. Member of the Crown Publishing Group.

Random House, Inc. New York, Toronto, London, Sydney, Auckland

http://www.randomhouse.com/

HARMONY and colophon are trademarks of Crown Publishers, Inc.

Design by Lynne Amft

Printed in the United States of America

Library of Congress Cataloging-in-Publication Data is available upon request

ISBN 0-517-70668-7

10 9 8 7 6 5 4 3 2 1

First Edition

I'd like to dedicate this book to that thing that keeps a woman going just when she's ready to give up. No, not caffeine. I'm talking about faith. Faith is that bridge between wanting and having. Actually, it's not only the bridge, it's the car and the map, too. May you have faith in abundance.

Acknowledgments

I'd like to thank all those people with penises who generously shared with me their penis tips (so to speak) on what it takes to succeed in business, beginning first with my agent, Lydia Wills, who understands the ups and downs of penises like nobody else.

I'd also like to thank Jay Dubiner, Mark Fisher, David Fuhrer, Bryan Lurie, Greg Manicherian, David Mitchell, Eric Salmansohn, Rubin Salmansohn, and Adam Taylor (NOTE: Those names are in alphabetical order, not in size of penis order).

I'd like to thank Hilary Bass and Amy Boorstein, two Amazon Girls at Crown who helped to make this penis book come alive.

Finally, I'd like to give a huge, long, firm thanks to my ballsy editor, Sherri Rifkin, for her wisdom, support, and that thing I mentioned in my dedication: her faith.

Contents

NOTE: The reference to a "penis" throughout this book is a purely fictional penis. Any resemblance to actual penises, living or dead, is entirely coincidental.

NOTE: According to Law #476 of the penile code, no penises were hurt or killed in the making of this book.

Live Now,
Procrastinate Later:
A Preface

*W*e all have it in us to get what we want. It's never too late to start on this path to change. It's never too late to get yourself that happy second childhood. And even after that, a happy third childhood. Or fourth childhood. Which reminds me of . . .

A Grim Wheelchair Analogy
(with a Happy Ending—Not to Worry)

You've read about them, I'm sure. I'm referring to those people who have been in accidents and told by doctors they'd be confined to a wheelchair for life. Then, within the year, they are up and walking to the kitchen for a few SnackWell's cookies. It's a miracle, these doctors say. Usually these people respond modestly, "Naah. I knew the doctors were wrong. I knew I'd be walking again." These people were determined to walk, to prove their doctors wrong. So they channeled all their inner energy into this goal, envisioned themselves walking, and did not give up. I say: If these folks, through sheer desire, will, and spirit, can make this happen, you, too, can do anything you want to do. Because you, too, have that same abundant desire, energy, will, spirit—whatever you want to label it as. It's all there inside you RIGHT now, just lying there dormant, a reservoir of untapped power that verges on the miraculous. And since (God willing) you don't need to expend this desire/energy/will/spirit learning to walk, you can channel it into your life goals, so you can soar.

You can do it. It's possible. To quote an underappreciated Zen philosopher, Bazooka Joe

"Your success is only limited by your desires."

— A B a z o o k a J o e c o m i c f o r t u n e

You just need to believe you can do it, to trust in yourself, and apply the secrets and strategies in the pages ahead. But that's just the tip of the penis. There's much much more to come. So read on.

— *How* —

TO SUCCEED
IN BUSINESS
WITHOUT
A PENIS

A WOMAN DOESN'T NEED A PENIS TO HOLD HER OWN: AN INTRODUCTION

I once joked to a client at MTV:

> *"My definition of comedy is when bad things*
> *happen to anyone who is* not *me."*

The next day I was reading a book on Taoism and discovered that I had unknowingly said a very Taoist thing. The Taoist approach to life's problems is to remove one's ego from a situation, which enables one to see life with more clarity and thereby learn more empowering lessons.

This ego-less approach matched up with my definition of comedy:

> *Anybody who is* not *me* = *a me that can detach*
> *my Velcroed-on ego from a dilemma.*

For me, laughter has always been therapeutic. Instead of living up to the expression "It only hurts when I laugh," I hurt when I *don't* laugh. And I hurt myself in the long run, too—because I don't learn nearly as much from the torture at hand if I don't step far enough away to be able to laugh at it.

What this means is: Because I believe humor is a good learning

1

aid, you'll find that *How to Succeed in Business Without a Penis* is not only a highly serious, helpful book for women in business, but also as a part of my goal of imparting twenty-twenty farsighted insights, it incorporates a humorous, irreverent viewpoint——as well as the gratuitous use of the word *penis*. (Sorry, Mom and Dad, about that last bit.)

I had toyed with the idea of telling my parents the book was called *How to Succeed in Business Without a Pianist*—and hoping they wouldn't notice. Or rewriting the title with a softer approach, say *How to Succeed in Business Without a Pee Pee.*

But in the end "Penis" won out.

But hey, doesn't it usually?

Can I confess something? I feel I'm ready to. Yes, there's nothing like using the word *penis* with a total stranger (that's you) to make me (that's me) feel all warm and fuzzy and comfortable about revealing secrets. So here's one now:

> *My use of the word* penis *is/was a highly strategic, manipulative attempt to get your attention.*

In other words:

> *I used to be in advertising.*

It's true. Before I became an author, I served time at major New York advertising agencies, including J. Walter Thompson, McCann Erickson, Young & Rubicam, and Avrett, Free, & Ginsberg, eventually becoming a twenty-something senior vice-president, Clio Awarded, monetarily rewarded creative director advertisingaholic. Then I went on to become an image consultant for L'Oreal, Revlon, MTV, E!, Nickelodeon, Comedy Central, Lifetime, Showtime, TNT, NBC, CBS, etc., etc., etc. (One of my goofier claims to fame was coining Burger King's "Croissandwich" as "The Croissandwich." My favorite name, "Whoppierre," was rejected.)

Although I was on the fast track, I was not happy or creatively sated writing commercials that got people all a-buzz about a *new! new! new! plaque-resistant, low-cholesterol, better-tasting floor wax!* I longed to write books that made people think and feel in new ways. Finally, at age twenty-eight, I felt old enough to know what I was doing if I quit—and young enough to still have the energy and idealism left in me to go out and really do it.

Plus, I've always believed that in life, we regret the things we *don't* do more than the things we *do.*

Plus, I've *also* always believed that it's not true we only get one life to live. We can live one to twenty-seven lives—*per lifetime.*

So I quit.

Like an indentured slave, I saved up enough money and bought my freedom. It was scary risking going from riches to rags, trying to make a career for myself as an author. But writing had always been my passion, and I believed—and still do—that my corporate background in advertising gave me an edge over most writers. After all, I had learned the difficult skill of climbing the corporate ladder in heels. Thankfully, this experience did come in handy—beginning with my very first book, *50% Off,* a novel.

The publication of *50% Off* was the best of times, worst of times. I quickly discovered it was a struggle to get publicity—which was crucial to sales—for a novel. Nonfiction books, I learned, were far easier to promote. *So . . .* with the aid of my advertising background, I repositioned my novel with a *nonfiction theme*: as a love guide for the nineties. Next, I applied my packaging/marketing skills to shameless self-promotion and positioned myself as a "Relationship Expert" in the hope of getting publicity for my novel. It worked. *Then . . .* this strategy worked *even better* for my second book, *How to Make Your Man Behave in 21 Days or Less, Using the Secrets of Professional Dog Trainers.*

Soon both books looked like they were going to be optioned for movies—"looked like" being the operative words. I spent a lot of time in L.A. (pitching TV shows, being offered development deals, taking

3

meetings), where I quickly learned Big Lesson #1: "Everybody Lies to Me. Trust No One," later to be followed by Big Lesson #2: "No More Ms. Nice Guy."

A Quickie Analogy of What I Went Through

It was as if I kept being told I had won an all-expenses-paid trip to Hawaii. Then, when I went to collect, I discovered I had merely won a sneakerphone.

I was growing jaded. And weary. My brother Eric suggested I read Sun Tzu's *The Art of War*. It changed my career life.

For those of you unfamiliar with Sun Tzu, he's the original Donald Trump of the Ancient China Warlord set. More than two thousand years ago, Sun Tzu wrote the ultimate war strategy guide, which has since been consulted by Samarais, Vietnam generals, communist leaders like Mao Zedong, modern-day executives, and at least one New York City writer—me—who reinterpreted *The Art of War* to apply to women in business in the nineties and repositioned it as *The Art of Wardrobe*, so to speak.

Soon after, my writer friend/colleague Susan asked me to guest-speak at one of her writing classes on marketing oneself as a writer. I discussed all I'd learned from Madison Avenue to L.A. to Sun Tzu. The seminar, according to Susan, was "TOTALLY LOVED" by her students. She asked me back the next semester. And the next. And the next. I did two more business seminars for other groups—one of them a women's group—where we discussed a variety of obstacles women face in business.

Which brings me once again to that "Penis Confession" I started earlier.

THAT PENIS CONFESSION
GROWS LARGER

*A*s I alluded to earlier, I used the word *Penis* in my book title because of my background in advertising/marketing. I know: The nineties marketplace is stupendously competitive. Books need to go that extra distance to stand out on the shelves.

The same goes for women.

Women must learn how to go that extra distance to stand out in the competitive career marketplace. It's hard enough to succeed in business *with* a penis these days, let alone without one. Especially with all the downsizing. Though I believe downsizing will be worse for the penises out there than for women. (Pardon the penis/downsizing inference.) After all, in the waters of a smaller work environment, a bad relationship creates larger reverberating waves, so a more intimate workplace can thereby benefit greatly from a woman's innate empathy and maternalistic people skills.

In fact, I believe many of a businesswoman's perceived disadvantages can *actually* serve as career advantages.

In other words, a woman doesn't need a penis to succeed in business. Though she does need balls. Also a good set of boobs doesn't hurt either. (Well, except sometimes.) Basically, every businesswoman needs to learn how to juggle all four entities: balls and boobs. Not an easy balancing job to attempt. Even for a female senior VP. *Especially* for a female senior VP. BUT it can be done—and without us women having to sacrifice our femininity. We don't have to make a choice:

Feminine or successful?
Pick one.

One of my goals in this book is to show how we women should not fight our female side, but rather learn to use it in our fight to attain career advancement.

5

A PIQUE PREVIEW

𝓘 have what I call a "wait problem." I hate to wait. In restaurants, I want my table *now*. In dieting, I want my size-four results *now*. In book writing, I want to tell you *everything*—well, you know. My favorite time of day is *now*.

Although this section that you are now reading is meant to serve mainly as an "Introductory Preface," I'm very eager to share some of my specific helpful business secrets and strategies that are coming up.

Like *now*.

The goal I mentioned above, not fighting our female side, is mainly discussed in the third part of this book, entitled "Support for Boobs in Business," in which I list ten female qualities I strongly believe should NOT be viewed as inequalities. For instance: Mommy Momentum, Cleavage Power, Advanced Romance Skills, Asking Indirections, and Evelyn Wood People-Reading Skills.

My guess is that some of you (particularly the men some of you— though why you are reading this particular book I have no idea) might find some of my secrets/strategies a little "provocative." But I know at least three men who will agree with me about how we women should be using our feminine powers—and even wiles—to our utmost advantage.

1. Sun Tzu. He said:

> *"Turn your own disadvantages into advantages*
> *and the enemies' advantages into disadvantages."*

2. Tolstoy. He said:

> *"Use whatever power you are served."*

3. Machiavelli. He said:

> *"David offered Saul to go and fight Goliath the*
> *Philistine champion, and Saul, to inspire him*

with courage, gave him his own weapons and
armour. Having tried these on, David rejected
them, saying that he would be unable to fight
well with them, and therefore he wanted to face
the enemy with his sling and knife. In short,
armour belonging to someone else either drops
off you or weighs you down or is too tight."

So you should not only rely on your female qualities, but only on those that you feel most comfortable with.

A COMMERCIAL BREAK

*B*asically, the secrets and strategies ahead are based on what is called in the advertising business:

Product Repositioning

One of the goals of Product Repositioning is to determine a consumer's potential negative response to your product, then turn your product's weakness into a perceived strength—or distract the consumers with an even more exciting apparent benefit. For instance:

1. Don't think of Arm & Hammer baking soda only as a good refrigerator deodorizer—think of it *also* as a great all-natural toothpaste.
2. Don't think of our candy as a fattening junk food. Think of it as "FAT FREE" and/or "LOW CHOLESTEROL" Or better yet as "La Junque Foode."
3. Don't think of women as "overly emotional," but rather think of them as having "more in-depth emotional capacities," which serve them well when it comes to "empathy" and "intuition" and "people-reading skills" and "being more self-aware and thereby

more capable of self-improvement on the job"—all traits that are stressed as essential ingredients for success in Daniel Goleman's ground-breaking book *Emotional Intelligence: Why It Can Matter More than IQ*.

In the upcoming sections, I will offer many secrets/strategies for the working/overworking woman that borrow heavily from the major advertising agencies' secrets/strategies for Product Repositioning. In a sense, we women are selling ourselves to a target audience called "Corporate America." Our main mission: to better understand what motivates this target audience into making a buying decision.

Translation: to better understand what motivates an employer into making a "hiring decision" or a "raise decision."

After all, once you understand your target audience's motivations, you can sell them nearly anything. Product Repositioning keeps this in mind—as well as the competition factor. It's also important to consider why someone would choose your product over its competitor—which, in a businesswoman's case, often means "men."

Coming up, you'll learn how to position yourself competitively with men by subliminally and overtly promising employers the same top male skills—only better. *And* you'll learn how to create the most alluring "packaging" and "pricing" for yourself to ensure you will stand out and be respected.

Advertising agencies have spent millions of dollars researching the best ways to go about Product Repositioning. Now you can find all their high-priced secrets in the upcoming sections— for the mere $21.00 purchase price of this book. (Yes, as I said, I used to be in advertising.)

Another goal for this book was to make it smarter than I was when I got the book deal. So I read everything in sight, and gleaned every tip there was on how to get to the highest rung—not the middle or upper-middle rung —of the career ladder.

Then I made "Karen Stew."

First I mixed together a wide variety of tips from my favorite writers, philosophers, and comic minds—then I stirred things up a bit by giving it all a female perspective.

My objective was to create a business book that is not only highly informational (as so many of the men's business books I read were) but also affirmational (as so many of the female business books I read were), knowing that in business it takes both a strong dose of perspiration *and* aspiration to get anywhere.

A N Y Q U E S T I O N S ?

*T*hough I hate to admit it, there is the possibility that you will not agree with every single philosophy and tip in my book. If not, that's okay. In fact, it's a good sign. It's great to question what you read and hear. That's also one of my philosophies for the workplace. Many things you're told in business should *not* be taken at face value,—but rather at two-faced value. I invite you to underline the parts of my book you disagree with, scribble questions in the borders, discuss your disgust with a friend over dinner, and/or write me care of Harmony Books. Always question motives. And question what works best for you—your particular needs. Not everything works for everybody—or every Buddha. As the Buddhists say:

> *"Do not blindly believe what others say. See
> for yourself what brings contentment, clarity,
> and peace. That is the path for you to follow."*

But also keep in mind what Shunryu Suzuki said:

> *"In the beginner's mind there are
> many possibilities, but in the expert's mind
> there are few."*

9

I promise you that if you keep an open, beginner's mind and follow the secrets/strategies laid out in this book, you will ABSOLUTELY find yourself better prepared, empowered, and focused—everything you need to achieve your career goals. I absolutely believe that with a healthy combo of knowledge, discipline, ingenuity, patience, practice —and, of course, a sense of humor—it's possible for a woman to succeed in a man's world, and receive equal opportunity and pay, instead of just equal ulcers.

As they say in L.A.: Trust me on this.

Except I really do mean it. But you know what? You don't even have to trust me. What I'm getting at is, all you need is to *trust yourself.* In fact, this "self-trust" is the primary trust fund you should be building. Once you trust your innate talents, you'll find you can open any and all of those closed office doors—without ruining your manicure or using a penis for leverage.

I believe you can do anything you have a passion for, if you put your mind to it. It's when others make you feel you can't that you can't.

— *Part 1* —

BELONGING TO

A CLUB THAT

WON'T HAVE

YOU WITHOUT

A MEMBER

—

THE OTHER
"PETER" PRINCIPLE

*R*ecently my buddy David got mugged at a bank machine by a beautiful, leggy woman.

"Actually, it might have been a transvestite," David corrected himself.

"It's okay if it was a woman," I told him.

"Actually," David said, now embarrassed, "the more I think about it, the more I'm sure he was a transvestite."

For me this story represents a lot about what's going on with women and men in the business world in the nineties. Men still don't expect women to have savvy, "chutzpah," and power. That's one of the reasons David got himself mugged in the first place—and one of the reasons women can succeed in business without a penis.

Because many men don't expect aggressive maneuvers from women —especially confident, attractive women—they're vulnerable to being overpowered, at both bank machines and bank boardrooms alike. As Sun Tzu explained in *The Art of War*:

> *"A commander who knows how to employ*
> *surprise attacks is like heaven and earth—*
> *infinite in transformations."*

This "sex change midstory" story also shows how many men have a difficult time accepting women who do have power—particularly power that exceeds and thereby supersedes men's power. Heck, my buddy David couldn't even accept a little female power from a low-end career like "mugger."

We've also seen this grumbly attitude on occasion in sports. Many guys have an admittedly difficult time being beaten by a woman in tennis—or even Ping-Pong. It thereby makes sense that a woman who surpasses men in the work force might also face some repercussions— and it also makes sense that men might face some repercussions from these repercussions.

For a while now there's been a shifting of the gears of power between men and women. As we women are growing stronger and more assertive, men are reacting by growing more afraid and threatened— making women react by feeling the need to grow stronger and more assertive. The result:

1. Scared, reticent, overly sensitized men
2. Frustrated, confused, pissed-off women

All this eagerly sought equality has brought us:

Equal neuroses for everyone!

In the pursuit of finding a fair balance of power, many men and women have assumed each other's *worst* traits rather than each other's *best* traits.

A N I M A / A N I M U S / E N E M I E S

*C*arl Jung wrote about how each of us has a male and a female side, called the anima and animus. As a woman gains more power in business, her male animus increases, which means that her internal balance of anima/animus shifts, which leads to a shift in the balance of power between her and a man (with his own internal anima-animus dynamic). This shifting is not only taking place in the interactions between an individual woman and man but also collectively between women and men. On the whole, the dynamics of the relationship between the sexes in our society is being thrown out of whack.

We women must take responsibility for our part in this.

Many women, out of insecurity about their newfound power, as well as fear of attack for attaining this power and, while we're at it, *actual* attack for attaining this power, are reacting and overreacting by drawing more and more from their male side for protection. For example: There are some women who mistakenly believe that succeeding in business requires imitating men—and even more mistakenly: stupid, obnoxious men.

For the Record

Even though I believe a woman doesn't need a penis to succeed, I do not recommend trying it without a heart or a brain.

Career women must be aware of not overreacting with aggression to the "repercussions" with which men have been known to challenge us. That should be our role in this male/female deal. Agreed?

Men, for their part, must learn to be more aware of the repercussions with which they are either consciously or unconsciously frustrating/torturing women. I am referring to all the stuff in the upcoming pages that is making businesswomen what we are today: overworked, underpaid, overwhelmed, and undersexed.

FROM CONFORMING TO GLASS SLIPPERS TO CONFORMING TO GLASS CEILINGS

Remember that Virginia Slims ad slogan about having come a long way, baby?

As I mentioned before, I believe it's good to question things. So I ask: How far have we women *really* come—especially when you consider that that expression includes the word *baby,* which instantly makes it condescending and thereby paradoxical?

I *also* have a few more questions.

A Few More Questions

1. Why is it that, according to a 1995 study conducted by the Glass Ceiling Commission, women still hold only 5 percent of top management positions in American corporations?
2. Why is it that of the seventy new women who joined the Fortune 1000 board in 1994, more than half were first-time board members?
3. Why is it that although women represent over half of the country, as of 1995, only 8 percent of congressional representatives are female? (Maybe we women shouldn't call this country the "US" but the "THEM.")
4. Have we women really seen advances in business—besides the advances made on us by male bosses?
5. Have we really been privy to change—besides the chump seventy-one-cent change women still receive to a man's dollar?
6. Why don't women command higher salaries than men when we've got more expensive upkeep: our haircuts, beauty toiletries, tailoring, dry cleaning, clothing, and skimpy bathing suits?
7. Which reminds me: Why are women still being charged more

than men for haircuts, beauty toiletries, tailoring, dry cleaning, clothing, and skimpy bathing suits?

Lack of equal salary and status are not a businesswoman's only disappointments. Many women have pursued careers with high expectations of living a fuller, richer life, with equal focus on both family and self-evolvement. Instead, many women have wound up with the *worst* of both worlds.

Too many women are being screwed at the office and not at home.

Let me state, right here, right now, although I *don't* believe you need a penis by day at the office to find happiness, that *doesn't* mean you should go completely without one by night.*

In her 1989 play *The Heidi Chronicles*, Wendy Wasserstein suggested that the more a woman's career succeeds, the more her chance for a happy family life recedes. Unfortunately, much hasn't changed in the 1990s.

Instead of our relationships being like that TV show:

Mad About You

They're more like:

Mad At You

I AM W O M A N.
I AM I N V I N C I B L E.
I AM M A J O R L Y B U M M E D.

*Y*ou know that expression:

You can never be too rich or too thin.

*NOTE: I don't mean to imply by the title of my book that I find the concept of penises as a category totally obsolete.

That's unfortunately all too true for women. Well, except for the rich part. At least, according to men. Many men have a reaction to highly successful, six-figured women. In a word:

Flaccid

Take my friend Missy—and she'd sure like to be taken—in every sexual sense of that expression. Missy, a successful real-estate broker, makes a lot more money than her now ex-boyfriend, a struggling actor. "When I was with him, I felt guilty that my career was going so much better than his," Missy says. "I never used to allow myself to fully celebrate my accomplishments, because I didn't want him to feel bad. Nor did I bring up any of the problems I was having. My problems didn't feel as important as his. Then, on top of all this, I'd allow him to make fun of my career. Bizarre, huh? When our sex life disappeared, well, I knew our relationship was in total trouble."

Many men are intimidated by women who have made it instead of mated. Many men will argue otherwise—that they want a woman who's intelligent, successful, and funny. But I could—and *will*—argue right back that for some men that's only as long as the woman's not *more* intelligent, *more* successful, and *more* funny. You know that expression:

Less Is More

That seems to be especially true when it comes to a man's response to a woman. It's the ol' "Smart Women, No Choices." With its sequel: "A Mute Girl Is a Cute Girl."

Doubt me? Give a guy a choice between dating the following:

1. A supermodel
2. A super conversationalist

Stumped as to which one he'll pick? Well, let's just say there's a reason the expression

spinster supermodel

is not as prevalent in our culture as

unmarried intelligent career woman.

I personally know a lot in the latter group, women I have termed "Amazon Girls": females with impressive internal strength and highly developed intellectual and monetary powers.

A QUICKIE STORY

*R*ecently a male friend, Larry, told me: "Karen, you are an ambitious woman."

I paused, then said, "Thank you?"—with that question mark firmly in place.

I didn't know. Is that word *ambitious* supposed to be connotation-free? Because I feel as if there's a connotation attached to that word—at least for a woman. Watch how that word changes like one of those Magic Eye posters:

LARRY IS AN AMBITIOUS MAN.

KAREN IS AN AMBITIOUS WOMAN.

The first is a total compliment. The second is . . . . well, for a woman it's a Thank You with a Question Mark. Then there are all the adjectives a woman gets called that are just plain No Thank Yous.

VOCABULARY LESSON #1

A woman is called:

AGGRESSIVE instead of ASSERTIVE

NAGGING instead of COMMUNICATIVE

BITCHY instead of PROACTIVE

OVERLY SENSITIVE instead of PUNCTILIOUS
OVERREACTING instead of JUST PLAIN REACTING
A BALL BUSTER* instead of CONFIDENTLY
DETERMINED

VOCABULARY LESSON #2

I've also noticed another strange, goofy thing about our American vocabulary. We assign positive attributes onto men's body parts:

BALLS

COCKSURE

COCKY

*CAJONES***

But we only have negative attributes for women's body parts:

BOOB

BUSHED

PUSSY

And for that matter, why don't we have expressions like:

VAGINA-SURE

IT TOOK A LOT OF CLIT TO ASK FOR THAT RAISE.

---

*Actually, what is a ball buster but a girl who fights balls with balls?

**Then there's the word *happiness,* which has the word *penis* hidden within it: "hap-penis." This was pointed out in the movie *Last Tango in Paris* by Marlon Brando—talk about a "hap-penis."

WOODY EXPLAINS THE "WOODY" PHENOMENON

*W*oody Allen said in his play *Central Park West*, "People don't hate you for your weaknesses, they hate you for your strengths." I believe that to be true—except they *also* hate you for your weaknesses. Especially if you're a woman. Women lose both ways. And because a woman's strength is what intimidates and thereby bothers a man most, that's where he'll kick a woman when she's up.

KICKING A WOMAN IN HER BALLS

*O*ften what it requires to become successful is taking an aggressive, proactive stance. Meaning? Bearing balls. Unfortunately, bearing balls often means risking losing one's lovability. For women, this can be a difficult loss. Women place a higher value on intimacy than men. (Michael Ovitz surely knows nobody is *ever* going to describe him as "adorable." My guess is he's sleeping just fine.)

Succeeding in business means constantly deciding between:

1. Winning
2. Being liked

It's a no-brainer for men. They'll choose winning. Men know:

Nice guys finish last.

Whereas many women are torn, because women don't know if:

1. Nice gals finish last.
2. Tough gals finish most last.

After all, we have that intimacy/loss thing to contend with.

Here's the double rub. In the end, ballsy men who choose winning over anything/everything/everyone *will still be liked anyway.* Because for men:

> *Winning = being liked.*

Whereas for a woman—even an adorable, lovable one—success can be its own revenge. Because for women:

> *Winning = being intimidating, stirring up jealousy, and creating a larger ratio of the wrong version of love letters: interoffice memos.*

Unfortunately, many women care about others' opinions of them. Whereas men innately understand what Machiavelli understood:

> *"It is far better [for a leader] to be feared than loved if you cannot be both."*

Or to put it another way—also a way the fun-loving Machiavelli put it:

> *"Some of the things that appear to be virtues will, if [a leader] practices them, ruin him, and some of the things that appear to be vices will bring him security and prosperity."*

Or to put it *my* way:

> **"Until a woman can change her un-evil ways, and be tough, bear balls, face controversy, and STOP caring what people think, then others— both men and women others—will forever have an edge over her in business."**

EVEN THE GUY WHO
INVENTED FIRE WAS FIRED

*A*s you can see, it's not enough for a woman just to have balls to succeed in business. She also needs good protective gear for them. Even in caveman's times, it wasn't much easier to make a mark for yourself. As Ayn Rand explains:

> *"Thousands of years ago the first man discov-*
> *ered how to make fire. He was probably burned*
> *at the stake he had taught his brothers to light.*
> *He was considered an evildoer who had dealt*
> *with a demon mankind dreaded. But thereafter,*
> *men had fire to keep them warm, to cook their*
> *food, to light their caves. He had left them a*
> *gift they had not conceived, and he had lifted*
> *darkness off the earth. . . . Every great new*
> *thought was opposed. Every great new inven-*
> *tion was denounced."*

There are many examples of society's opposition to fresh, original thinking. Two that immediately come to mind are:

1. Albert Einstein
2. The TV game show *Family Feud*

First, let's consider Albert's situation. Einstein, for the first chunk of his life, was thought to be a total lunatic. In school a teacher even described him as "adrift forever in his foolish dreams." Guess she was wrong.

Next, let's take a look at that popular TV game show.

The goal in *Family Feud* was to test how much a contestant could think *like everyone else.* The more your answers matched up with *every-*

body else's, the more cash and prizes you were rewarded. Conversely, those individuals who thought like individuals and had unique answers were rewarded with guffaws. Interestingly, the American public rewarded this show with extremely high ratings.

These mere two examples say plenty about our society's attitudes toward the free, original thinker.

And speaking of *Family Feud,* that reminds me of another important societal pressure women have to deal with. . . .

WE INTERRUPT YOUR REGULAR PROGRAMMING

*A*lot of a businesswoman's problems begin with her childhood programming. Many girls don't have upbringings but "downbringings."

It's like this: While boys are given sports equipment to get in training for "The Little Leagues," girls are given dolls to get in training for "The Love Leagues"—or rather "The *Unrequited* Love Leagues." A little girl who plays with dolls is actually practicing loving and caring for an inanimate object that will give nothing back.

She is taught the glory of selflessness—to care about others before caring about her own ego gratification, to put her own happiness and needs in:

Second place

A little boy, on the other hand, doesn't give anything to his baseballs, basketballs, footballs, volleyballs.* Sports equipment gives to a boy instead of vice versa, further defining a boy's sense of self, feeding his ego. His goal in sports is to be:

Number one

---

*Just think up any word with "balls" in it, and it will relate back to guys.

Actually, a boy's games do more than feed his ego: They provide a veritable ego feast. A little boy is encouraged to pig out on ego sustenance, by screaming loudly, showing off, bragging, getting dirty, and running wild, whereas a little girl's games provide nouvelle cuisine portions of ego sustainers. She's told to stay neat, quiet, modest, demure. Be a nonaggressive little lady. The only thing a little girl is fed in large portions is humble pie. Unfortunately, you are what you *don't* eat.

During the teenage years, these smaller portions continue to be doled out to girls, while a teenaged boy is allowed to play, play, play outside his house until late at night and to explore his sexuality. The typical teenaged girl, however, has a curfew on her playtime, and a potential stigma hovering over her head should she act on her appetites (i.e., play with anything a "nice" girl should not be playing with). Basically, females are taught to show self-restraint in all ego-gratifying areas: sex, food, conversation. And this Kate Moss Ego Diet Plan is carried over into adulthood.

RADIO ACTIVE MEN

*W*hen I did radio call-in shows for my book *How to Make Your Man Behave in 21 Days or Less Using the Secrets of Professional Dog Trainers*, mostly only guys called in. I was surprised. I felt my book would certainly attract many female callers. The host explained that, regardless of the subject, the ratio is always skewed toward male callers. I suppose this is a trend that starts in grade school. Studies show that boys are called on more in class, and as a result tend to raise their hands more. Studies also show that later in life big boys continue to talk more than women in group discussions—which is ironic when you consider that women have a reputation for talking so much. (I'll explain why this is in Part 2.)

KEEPING DOWN WITH THE JONESES SYNDROME

*B*ecause of childhood programming, all women have a potentially dangerous enemy at the office. No, not those people who crush beer cans with their heads. No, I'm talking about:

A woman's superego

It can often be found working overtime: taming a woman's drive for power, attention, and money; worrying about what people think; feeling fearful and guilty over making friends jealous about her success—and thereby attempting to *Keep Down with the Joneses.*

In contrast, a guy has a majorly helpful work assistant:

A man's Super Ego

It consistently roots him on to get more, more, more—and compliments him on a job well done, often before he's done it, and even if nobody else thinks he's done it well.

So, while a woman's superego is constantly whispering:

Watch out! Less is more!

. . . a man's Super Ego is busy screaming:

Watch out, world! More is More! I want a beer!

Guess who winds up with more raises and more beer?

GUILTING THE LILY

*G*irls are trained to have an extra talent boys aren't: the talent for guilt. Because as little girls we experienced being kept down or kept out (or kept down and out), we know better what it's like as big girls when a friend or coworker feels as if he or she is being kept down or kept out (or kept down and out).

On the one hand, this means big girls have better "empathy skills." But then there's that other hand, which can often be found strangleholding a big girl's ambition: the grasp of guilt.

Psychologists have their own clinical term and explanation for this response:

Masochistic Equilibrium

Briefly, what this means is that in childhood, some of us grow up with a 90 percent familiarity with happiness, others with only 75 percent. When this concentration shifts—even if it's *upward*, increasing our happiness—we feel the imbalance, and long to shift the level back to our comfort zone—even if it's *downward*, away from more happiness.

For instance, there are cases of people who win gazillions of dollars in the lottery but suffer the unfortunate fate of not ever feeling comfortable about spending their award money. So it just sits under their mattress. If you are one of these people, I have a helpful suggestion. Send *me* the money care of Harmony Books. If you don't feel comfortable sending money through the mail, then just keep in mind that I'm a size six. And this is one time you shouldn't ask questions. Just do it.

WOMEN ARE WORRIERS. MEN ARE WARRIORS.

A woman's superego has many ways to accomplish its anti-accomplishment goal. The obvious:

Procrastination and not using spellchuck

The less obvious:

Perfectionism

How's that? Because basically perfectionism is but a euphemism for "fear and procrastination." (And in the spirit of procrastination, I'll explain that concept further to you LATER, on page 127. No, give me until page 131. You know what? Make that page 140. But I mean it. On page 140—or rather 140-ish.)

Women waste a lot of mental energy and time caught up in worries and fears—as well as a Whitman's Sampler of emotional responses to all the politics being played out at the office. Men, however, don't do this nearly as much. As Don Juan once said:

> *"The basic difference between an ordinary man*
> *and a warrior is that a warrior takes every-*
> *thing as a challenge, while an ordinary man*
> *takes everything as a blessing or a curse."*

Women have to learn how to be better warriors. Basically, men are better at handling the remote control not only on their TV sets *but also* on their mind-sets. Whereas women tend to rewind to mistakes and insecurities, and replay them over and over again, men switch channels until they find something enjoyable.

Mostly, men know not to waste valuable energy and time caught up in negative emotions. They know instinctively that this will only deplete and distract them from their goal. And men in business have one goal only:

Win

This single goal focus is CRUCIAL if you ever want to become a millionaire, gazillionaire, famous artist, poor but respected artist, CEO, top assistant to CEO—pick your definition of success.

As the accomplished poet Maxine Kumin once said:

"God serves the choosy, they know what they want."

Or as Ralph Waldo Emerson put it:

"A man becomes what he thinks about most of the time."

Unfortunately, the hardest part of this task is not the "thinking about it" part, but the part before that, where you first determine what it is you want to become. In other words, before you can get to:

Win

you must first answer the question:

Win what?

In the Question Business this is what is called a "Trick Question," because all too often your first answer is the wrong answer.

H O L Y   G R A I L
O R   H O L Y   B R A I L L E ?

*I*t's been said: Love is blind. That especially applies to our "career loves." In other words, we are blind to what drives us—meaning we are driving blindly—meaning we could be careening dangerously down the wrong career path. I, however, have a good "Beginner's Driving Test" to determine if you have the vision needed to handle those dangerous curves on the road to success.

First, tell me. You can be honest. Am I overusing those driving analogies? I am, aren't I? I promise that was my last one.

ANYWAY . . . The test is to fill in the blank below:

BIRDS GOTTA FLY.
FISH GOTTA SWIM.
SERIAL KILLERS GOTTA KILL.
I'VE GOTTA _____.

I know, I'm picking an odd time to be making jokes. After all, the answer to the question "I want to WIN WHAT?" is probably one of the most serious and life-determining questions you will ever ask yourself. The answer to this question will determine the tone and shape and happiness quotient of the rest of your life.

No wonder we spend more time thinking about what we should have for dinner—Chinese or Italian.*

It's odd when you consider that many of us left the choice of our careers in the hands of some eight-year-old kid, because many of us decided in our childhoods what we wanted to do when we grew up. In keeping with the above restaurant analogy, what career you what to go into is even harder to know in advance than knowing on Tuesday if you'll want to eat Italian on Saturday.

Face it. A lot can happen in a couple of decades. Most likely you've changed since you were a teenybopper—especially your bopper, which is probably not so teeny anymore. You've probably also updated your drink of choice from milk to tequila sunrises to beer to wine to Seagram's to milk of magnesia. It's about time you updated your career goal as well.

Unfortunately "I want to win what career goal?" is a far scarier question than "I want to eat what for dinner?" But it is unquestionably a question worth taking the time to answer.

If possible, that answer should be narrowed down to one simple sentence. These concentrated words will help you concentrate better on

---

*NOTE: When in doubt, go Mexican.

making success-oriented decisions, not only in the long run about which career you should be pursuing, but even day to day, hour to hour, minute to minute as far as handling specific targeted work decisions.

MISSION POSSIBLE

*I*n advertising, I used to spend a lot of time writing for products what is called:

A Mission Statement

All ads for a product—even coupon ads—had to conform to this mission statement. It kept campaigns focused and thereby helped a product maintain its brand identity in that confusing and competitive maelstrom called the consumer marketplace. Because the career marketplace is just as chaotic, I recommend you write your own mission statement to keep you on track.

Don't panic if you don't know what your mission statement (a.k.a. career goal) is right away. I have some exercises to help you firm one up. And don't panic if you dread the words *exercise* and *firm up*. None of this requires getting into embarrassing spandex gear or listening to disco music about men raining from heaven. I wouldn't do that to you. After all, I want you to save up your energy. You'll need as much of it as you can muster to pursue this new mission statement of yours.

SCORING GOALS

*I*n the career world, a mission statement is composed of two different kinds of goals: inner and outer. A big mistake some folks make is picking an outer career goal without first considering one's inner career goals. For instance, kids often pick becoming a "fireman" or "ballerina"

31

because these jobs sound cool and impressive, without considering their own true inner talents and desires. Outer goals usually eventually fade away because they're not based on satisfying inner passions but on outer passing trends. Unfortunately, some of us are still picking outer goals for our career goals—and for the same ego-based (and base) reasons.

So be careful not to answer "Win what?" based on:

I think I should be a _____.

Instead, you should base it on:

I feel as if I already am a _____ waiting to happen.

You should not be basing your career goal on what you *think* you want to be, or what your parents think you want to be, or what your paramour thinks you want to be, BUT on *what you really, really, really want to be.* You must learn to please yourself—or rather *yourselves,* all those different hungry internal parts of you—with the exclusion of your ego.

One of the tempting outer career goals people can get confused about and start to pursue is "I Want to Become a Person Who Makes Wads and Wads of Money." Cash has this hypnotic power that can make people forget their real desires—or misinterpret "real desires" to mean desiring *real* Rolex watches or *real* Prada bags. It's funny how some folks can even tell the difference between a real Prada bag and a fake Prada bag, but not a real Prada bag and a real desire. Go figure.

Another seductive outer career goal people can get suckered into pursuing is "I Want to Become a Person with Lots of Status and/or Fame Who Doesn't Have to Wait in Line at Crowded Restaurants." This outer career goal is getting more and more popular as time goes on —as Andy Warhol first predicted, and the popularity of TV talk shows later proved accurate. I once heard this great quote:

"It used to be important people are famous, now famous people are important."

32

This statement reminded me of something I actually once heard someone say at a party: "I want to be famous—I just don't know for what yet."

You're heading in the wrong direction if you're thinking like the person above—or if your present idea of success is to have a vitamin shaped in your image, or to be known simply by your first name, like Cher, Madonna, Lassie . . . or God.

My Defaming Theory on Fame

I do not recommend pursuing any kind of outer career goal over an inner one. In the end it will always be self-defeating because it will never be self-satisfying. I know.

I admit that for a while, in my attempt to sell books so I could survive as an author, I got caught up in TV appearances and momentarily forgot why I was doing TV appearances in the first place: so I could survive as an author. I needed to remember that writing was my real inner desire. I did not crave being a glib TV personality but rather longed to be an author who shared philosophies (and a few good laughs at this ridiculous thing called life) that might help others think and grow in new ways. This inner goal applied to myself as well. I had wanted to write books to help me grow and think more, too.

Okay, so that's me, and my true inner career goal.
Now what about you?

PLAY NOW, WORK LATER

*F*inding your career goal is a lot like playing that game from childhood:

Where's Waldo?

Waldo was hiding somewhere in a complicated chaotic scene, like a picnic in Central Park or my office during an important work deadline. ANYWAY . . . The goal was:

Find Waldo.

This is also the first and most difficult step to improving your career life. *First* you have to find Waldo, which in Career Metaphor Land . . .

Career Waldo = inner *career goal/mission statement.*

(NOTE: Hereafter I will use the phrase "Career Waldo" in reference to your *inner* career goal/mission statement.)

This Career Waldo, like the real Waldo, is never out in the open, but cleverly concealed inside something else. Usually the inner regions of your heart—a place more women tend to look than men. *Therefore, more women than men are better at finding their Career Waldos.*

Men, as a crowd, are an externally oriented bunch. They're more into the things you can touch, whereas women are more into the things you can feel. I'm not sure if this is because of—or leads to?—men's acknowledged three-dimensional spacial-relations talent. In spacial-relations tests, men repeatedly prove superior at recognizing, envisioning, and understanding the three-dimensional aspects of this world. I believe this might be why men don't bother—as much as women—to consider the nondimensional, internal world of emotions, because people in general shy away from things they're not good at.

We women, however, are innately more talented at analyzing feel-ings, so we are rewarded every time we plunder into our internal depths, and therefore are less afraid to look into these depths and find our Career Waldos—*the most important first step to improving one's career life.* Lucky, lucky us.

AN EXCERCISE BREAK

*O*kay. We're now ready. Remember I promised you some "exer-cises" to help you "firm up" your Career Waldo? Well, here they are. You'll find all bad exercise entendres are highly appropriate, because after both kinds of exercises, you will feel discomfort and fatigue. Which is good. It's a sign you're using new muscles, developing, getting stronger. I recommend you start off your office exercise regimen with what I call:

The Staremaster

So, how do you use this Staremaster? Simply *stare* at the following questions, then think long and hard about the answers. Then write your answers down in a journal. For an added positive motivational kick, entitle your journal "How I Got My Dream Job." If you've never kept a journal before, you'll find writing in one is especially therapeutic, because staring at a white page can be a form of meditation. I want you to do a lot of staring at a lot of white pages. Then fill them up, and later read them back. You'll see clusters of clues as to where you went wrong that you can learn from and that you can use to remind yourself how far you've come. But for now you'll be using your journal to record your answers to the following questions.

Put aside about an hour to use this Staremaster for the first time. Then you should go back to look at the answers you've written in your journal for a minimum of ten minutes daily for the next month. Feel free to change and/or update your answers as much as you like. Keep your journal handy while you are reading this book because later on I will refer you back to your answers and have you think about them in many different ways. You should also review your answers whenever you need to get pumped up for a particular business challenge.

Eventually, with the help of staring at this Staremaster, you will see a change. You won't develop:

buns of steel

but . . .

a will of steel

. . . which is a crucial muscle to develop if you plan to climb to the top of that corporate ladder. Ready? Grab your journal and let's begin. . . .

Staremaster
For Helping You
Master Your Career Waldo

Record your answers to the following questions in your journal:

1. **What would you do if you had limited time?** It can often help your career if you imagine you have only six months left to live. (Though sometimes it can *also* help to imagine that your evil boss has only six months left to live, thereby putting you in cheerier spirits.) Think up twenty-five things you'd do differently if you had only six months left. Then think up twenty-five things you'd do EXACTLY the same, without that six-month limit. Chances are you will have a hard time coming up with fifty things—which is the point. I want you to stretch your mind. If you push yourself, you'll discover things about yourself and your desires you kinda knew but never really

thought about. Compare your two lists. See how much of what you are presently doing is on your "Fatal Illness List." The more things that both lists share, the better. This means you're living your life to its filled-to-the-brim fullest.

2. **What would you do if you had unlimited time?** Imagine you could live to be three hundred years old—which means, while you're at it, you should imagine that melatonin REALLY worked because it wouldn't be much fun to live to three hundred if you had to have three-hundred-year-old wrinkles. But that's just one vain girl's opinion. ANWAY . . . Would you pick a different career if you thought you had more time to achieve your goals? List twenty-five things you'd do differently if you had more time. As you'll realize, this means you are being offered the opportunity to go back to school or have children a little later, two options you could *really* consider. This is the good news. You *do* have more time than you think—if you focus, prioritize, and simplify. This is such a universal truth that there's even something called the Paretor Principle, which contends that 80 percent of results flow out of 20 percent of the time spent doing something. Keep this in mind when you pick and choose what to do in a given busy day. We waste a lot of time. I know. At one point I was going to the gym for two hours daily, until I asked myself: "Do I want to be an aerobics instructor or a writer?" I chose the latter and cut back on the former.

3. **What are you doing when you have unlimited metaphysical time?** You know those moments in your life when "time flies" because you are in such bliss? What are you doing? Try to remember twenty-five times when this has happened. It could be while you were cooking or tending a garden or reading or writing. Whatever. These activities are your truest talents and most precious inner resources. If you don't use them, you are

37

displaying a poverty mentality of your talents, which is the equivalent of having money in the bank and frugally never enjoying it. Or . . . like having a safe-deposit box filled with incredible jewels but being afraid to wear them, so you settle for wearing lesser fake cheap zircon stuff all your life.

4. **What would you do if you had unlimited money?** If you already had a million dollars, what would you do for a living? The ideal goal is to find a job that you'd *still* be doing. As I mentioned, money should never be the sole object of your desire. (It's the cool things that you can get with money that should be—just kidding, just kidding.) But seriously, work involves five days out of seven in a week. That becomes five-sevenths of your life—and realistically that percentage could turn into six-sevenths—so you'd better enjoy what you do. Besides, I believe that if you waited to find a job you LOVE, you'd most likely make a lot of money ANYWAY. Instead of money bringing you happiness, I believe happiness will bring you money.

5. **What would you do if you had unlimited bravery?** If you weren't afraid to do it, what twenty-five things would you most enjoy doing on a daily basis? In your fantasy, dare to not care what people would say. Dare to gain weight. Next, ask yourself what twenty-five things you'd be afraid of IF you gained not only weight but lots of power and achieved your career goal. Usually this list includes: "People will be jealous of me and hate me." But remember: These *will* be the wrong people. Next, write a list of twenty-five psychic predictions of the psycho attacks others could make on you if you (1) tell them your dream goal and/or (2) achieve your dream goal. Then write a list of twenty-five rebuttals—so you'll be prepared.

6. **What would you do if the career world had unlimited opportunities?** Write a list of twenty-five jobs you'd pursue if

you didn't think they were in such competitive fields. The good news is: If you're good at what you do, these fields won't be so competitive. And if these jobs are rooted in your inner goals, chances are you *would be* good at what you do. Next, do some research about these fields, and try to figure out their related cousin careers—that is, careers that are sort of like the one you want, only different—and therefore less competitive. For instance, instead of pursuing commercial advertising, you could consider corporate advertising or medical product advertising. We live in a world of abundance. There are so many choices of things out there to do and be. (Or rather *be* and do.) Snapple comes in a hundred and twelve flavors. Life does, too.

7. **Reread your address book, and answer the following:** How many new names have you added in the last few years? How do these new people differ from your old friends? How have your friendships with your old friends changed throughout the years? Who do you feel less close to? Why? What qualities do most of your long-term friends have in common? What qualities do you avoid in people? Why? How do each of your friends see you differently—or do they? Do you act differently around your colleagues and work friends than you do with your nonwork friends? Which qualities do your work friends and nonwork friends have in common? Ideally, they should share similar qualities and values. List twenty-five new things you learn about yourself and your values from answering these questions.

8. **Why do lists always have to go up to ten?** Or five? What's wrong with having only eight items in a list, like this list has? That's right. Lucky you, you get to take the last two numbers off. Use the time to get a cup of coffee, then we'll come back and crack down again.

WHAT'S MY LINE?

*R*eady? You can wash that cup later. Let's move on.

Review all your answers, then organize on a new page of your journal all the qualities you listed that had to do with satisfying your *inner* world.

An Example

My inner-world goal:
I enjoy a creativity-filled, writing-filled, love-filled, laugh-filled, idea-filled life, meeting smart, interesting people, doing lots of traveling, while still finding time to buy vacuum-cleaner bags.

Next, brainstorm on how you can find an outer situation that will enable you to tap into these inner qualities. I came up with two solutions for myself.

For Example

My outer-world goal:
1. Write funny yet not too far from philosophical books—while hanging out in cafes, drinking too much coffee, bantering with smart, interesting freelance folks, and/or reading books when I'm not writing them.
2. Marry Andy Garcia.

Whereas your list of inner-goal qualities can and should be as long as possible, you should conversely try to narrow down your outer-goal list, and if possible just list one goal—and a short one at that. The narrower you define your outer career goal, the easier it will be for you to determine whether a specific job is right for you—and for you to appear right for the job. Once you define yourself, you can better position yourself to stand out in this competitive marketplace. In the world of advertising, this is called "niche positioning." And it works. Big-time.

I WAS A TEENAGE SWIMMING COCKTAIL WAITRESS

*E*ven before I was in advertising, I was intuitively destined for the business. In college I worked one summer as a cocktail waitress at the Tamiment Resort in the Poconos. It was a hot, hot summer. I had to work the poolside on blistering-hot days. Nearly all my potential drink buyers were wisely cooling off in the pool.

> *My problem:* I had hardly any drink buyers. I wasn't making any money. I was sweating and miserable.

My solution: I stripped down to my bathing suit, got into the cool, refreshing pool with tray and order pad, and took drink orders.

The result: My potential drink buyers loved the drink-ordering convenience as well as the playful absurdity of a swimming cocktail waitress. Everyone benefited. Particularly me. I made lots of money *and* got a nice, refreshing swim.

Later: I became known as "The Swimming Cocktail Waitress." In the resort's nightclubs, this new moniker served me well in my serving of drinks. Everyone wanted to order drinks from "The Swimming Cocktail Waitress."

Developing a niche also served me well in my subsequent careers —especially this one as an author. Because I've always loved making my female friends laugh about the relationship stuff that could get them so upset, I soon found myself channeling those instincts into my writing, and developed a niche as a writer for females. Because of this narrower focus, when MTV and Nickelodeon wanted to create TV shows for their female target audience, they thought of me. A more general writer might not have sprung as easily into their minds.

Taoism also supports niche marketing when it suggests:

> *"Concentrate all of your energy and*
> *intelligence on one thing."*

Once you've determined your career goal, you need to concentrate your energies to achieve it. You need a marketing plan. Look no further. *Voilà:*

Staremaster
Part Deux

A Career-Goal Marketing Plan

1. Write up a one-page pep talk for yourself on why you want your career goal, how great your life would be if you achieved it, and how much you deserve to achieve it. Psyche yourself up. Then whenever you get frustrated, reread what you've written.

2. Analyze in detail how to achieve your goal, breaking down and numbering the actions you must take so you can see clearly what the road ahead looks like. For instance, one of the things on your list might be: "Call Cousin Suzy, who knows someone who knows someone who knows Andy Garcia."

3. Organize a day-by-day, week-by-week, month-by-month schedule to help you accomplish the actions above. Make sure your monthly schedule includes a *balance* of work and play, or else you could get frustrated and give up. My girlfriend Shelley had a funny thing to say about balance: "There are some people who think a balanced life is about living moderately, then there

are others who think it means going from one extreme to the other extreme."

4. Mornings are the trajectory for your entire day. Be sure to begin your day in a pampering way. Take a long hot shower. Indulge in a cup of gourmet coffee. Flip through your favorite magazine or the newspaper. Write in your journal. Then, most important: Review your journal and remind yourself what your single goal focus is for that day.

5. Bedtime is an ideal time to review how your single goal focus for your day went. Figure out what you learned, what you accomplished, and what you still need to accomplish. Tell yourself a bedtime story in which you are the hero at the office in the days to come.

6. When you're at the office during the day, call your home answering machine and leave positive and complimentary messages for yourself to remind yourself how well you are doing at your career.

7. You can't get to the top of the career ladder if you're not in good health, so create a workout schedule for yourself and make sure you stick to a balanced diet.

8. Drink three tall glasses of water daily. The ventilation systems in many office spaces can be very dehydrating. A definite brain drainer.

9. Make a list of all your predictions of the obstacles you will face, then write how you will deal with them. By being prepared, you won't be caught off balance when difficulties do arise. Even better, decide how to avoid obstacles altogether. For instance, if you need more education, sign up for a class. Remember: More *learning* translates into more *earning*.

10. Head up an Energy Conservation Program. Figure out who and what in your life is zapping you of energy, then decide how to best deal with these situations.

11. Visualize end results. I did a lot of positive visualization when I was writing my first novel. One day I even went to a bookstore specifically with the goal of visualizing my novel on the bookshelf. I discovered I'd be next to Salinger—nice company to keep. Do the equivalent for your career goal. Visualization is definitely a powerful work aid. When you think about it, right now you are subconsciously visualizing yourself only getting to a certain level in your career—and you are making that a self-fulfilling prophecy. So why not raise your fantasy a notch, or even better, a million notches, and watch your reality follow?

12. Spend time with the elderly. If you don't have grandparents, sign up to help out at an old-age home. You'll learn wonderful life lessons—in particular, you'll be reminded that RISK IS WHERE IT'S AT IN LIFE. Regret eventually replaces fear and/or nostalgia.

13. Spend time with kids. If you or your friends/siblings don't have kids, sign up to volunteer at a day-care center. By talking to kids, you'll be reminded of the joys of spontaneity and the stress-freeness that lack of judgment can bring.

14. Clean out your closet. Often what keeps us from making life-improving changes is our attachments to the past. By cleaning out your closet you'll practice letting go of attachments—and witness how letting go can free up space to add newer, better, and more up-to-date things. Another metaphorical closet-cleaning lesson: You might already have some great things hidden away that you've forgotten about.

15. Okay, so you got off easy on the last list—but not this one. There is a fifteenth thing you must do. I want you to keep in mind: You can change your mind. Be open to updating your career goal. You might learn new things about the goal you've decided on that make you realize it's a poor choice. For

44

instance, you might have heard a rumor that Andy Garcia is already married. MY POINT IS . . . you and the world around you are constantly changing. It makes sense that your career goal might undergo change as well—and that's okay, just as long as this change doesn't come from lack of faith!

AN ORIGINAL FLAVORED GOAL WITH 100 PERCENT GUARANTEE

*B*y now, I hope, you have found your Career Waldo, organized a plan of action, cleaned out your closet, and called your Cousin Suzy to see if she knows anything about Andy Garcia's marital status.* Now what?

It's time to give your career goal the ol' road test. I know earlier I promised you no more driving analogies, but that was my last one. I really promise it this time.

Oh . . . and I'll also give you a guarantee. AND just for the record . . . I'm *not* one to make guarantees. In the advertising business, we are taught to think twice before making a guarantee. In fact, if you'll notice, I only "promised" not to make any more driving metaphors, I didn't guarantee it. But I WILL guarantee you this:

My 100 Percent Guarantee

You will be bombarded with a series of obstacles on your way to achieve your goal that will make you mutter: "I $#@!&% can't do this. I need a nap."*

---

*NOTE: If you *do* know anything about Andy Garcia's marital status, please write to me c/o Harmony Books.

Basically there are two obstacles you must look out for:

1. You
2. Everybody else

I'VE SEEN THE ENEMY AND SHE LOOKS JUST LIKE ME

The way nature goes through winter, spring, summer, and fall, so does our inner nature. When we are in our "fall" mode, we can lose faith that we'll ever see the sunlight of summer in our being, or that spring in our step.

I was in a "fall" mode last year. I sold a TV show, with a pilot script that I wrote and loved. *Then* the network started changing my script in a way that, well, I felt as if the show I was giving birth to was very "Rosemary's baby": frighteningly not mine anymore.

I started losing faith in ever achieving a satisfying writing career. My friend Sam was very helpful to me during this depressing time. He kept telling me, "Your day will come, Karen, your day will come." Which now that I think about it isn't so hot. I mean, I only get *one* day? After all I've been through, I think I've at least earned a fortnight. So let's forget what Sam said, and instead remember what Soen said:

> *"Ten years searching in the deep forest; today*
> *great laughter at the edge of the lake."*

You never know when/where you'll find your happiness. The search for attaining one's career goal is like the quest Patricia Arquette made Nicolas Cage go on to prove his love to her. I heard that Patricia gave Nicolas a list of things he had to bring her, stuff like an orchid plucked from a bush in Africa. You get the idea. ANYWAY, it's as if your career goal is testing your love for it as well, by putting

46

you through all sorts of trials and tribulations to prove how much you want it.

During these times that you are "being tested," you'll find it helpful to reread that Pep Talk page I made you write—and to think about the following analogy I used to help me finish my first novel.

It's Not Only a Rat Race Out There, But a Long-Distance Rat Race

Every time I thought I couldn't write another page, when I was ready to give up, I kept envisioning myself as a long-distance runner competing in a race, and I'd think: Right now, if I'm exhausted at this point, so are others, meaning right now another less determined writer is giving up, which means if I go on, the competition is less, and I'm getting closer to the winner's line. Then I'd force myself to go just a little farther—just to that "next tree." This is what you must do when you feel your faith collapsing: give yourself a "next tree" to get to.

Although I "promised" no more driving references, I will give you a quote from the man who made all driving references possible: Henry Ford. He said:

"If you believe that you can do a thing, or if you believe you cannot, in either case you are right."

Remember, every morning is a new beginning—and at least, thanks to your marketing plan, you are conscious of what it is you want to achieve each day, which is a big head start over a lot of other people. Speaking of you versus a lot of other people . . .

I'M OKAY,
EVERYBODY ELSE SUCKS

*O*kay, we've covered the obstacles you personally are responsible for setting up for yourself. That only leaves you with another 2 billion people's obstacles to deal with. Unfortunately, sometimes it can feel as if all these people are all working at the same office with you. Sometimes it can seem as if the world is a dark and dangerous place. Or in the words of Dorothy:

"Lions and tigers and bears, oh my!"

In Part 2, we will discuss a variety of methods for taming these lions and tigers and bears, using one-on-one techniques, but for now, I'd like to discuss some of society-as-a-whole's less obvious but just as dangerous forces that could make you question your faith, lower your confidence, and diffuse your energies.

HOLLYWOODN'T

*Y*ou can tell a lot about a culture by its mythologies. Our culture's main source for myths is Hollywood. I find it interesting (that's a euphemism for "it pisses me off") that the media's two biggest offerings on sexual harassment have been David Mamet's play-turned-movie *Oleanna* and Michael Crichton's book-turned-movie *Disclosure*. Both deal with women sexually harassing men. Yeah, like *that's* a big problem.

I also find it "interesting" that Hollywood is having a resurgence of sweet fluffy actresses like Alicia Silverstone and Sandra "Dee" Bullock who are getting all the guys and lead movie roles, thereby hurting my potential dating allure—as well as my potential movie star career.

And what's the story with the story in *Mrs. Doubtfire*? It portrays a busy career woman with no heart who doesn't evolve, and a man who in the end learns to balance both career and being a mom—an Über-Mom in the form of Mrs. Doubtfire in the form of *Mrs. I Doubt It Very Much*. In other words, *men* can master *both* career and family. For women it's another story—and a story that won't be filmed.

Lately we've also seen a slew of movies with women working as strippers and hookers: *Casino, Striptease, Showgirls, Leaving Las Vegas*—some "interesting" career choices to show women as having made it, huh?

And I'm sure you've already noticed how rarely—if ever—does Hollywood show a career woman who is actually good or has a happy work/family life—and is not murdered in the end. Instead we see the underwearless ice-pick queen Sharon Stone in *Basic Instinct* and the bunny-boiling Glenn Close in *Fatal Attraction*. Then there's the punished career mom in *The Hand That Rocks the Cradle*. Even in the empowering *Thelma and Louise*, the duo dies in the end—and so did the writer Callie Khouri's career. It took forever for Callie Khouri to get another movie made, then it barely got promoted. In 1995, Khouri wasn't even shown in *Vanity Fair*'s Hollywood Moguls issue in its double-page spread of writers—in fact, *no women* were shown.

Evidently there's been a negative societal reaction to all this Amazon Girl energy. The Hollywoodagram being sent to women reads:

Yo, girls. Make love, not money.

In a way, Hollywood is following a Machiavellian principle. In *The Prince*, he recommended a public punishing of those who are out of control, saying:

*"The brutality of this spectacle kept the people
of the Romagna for a time appeased and
stupefied."*

These punitive scenes are meant as a subliminal warning to ambitious women of men's ultimate reign.

WOMEN WHO RUN WITH THE NAOMI WOLFS

*T*here's been a history of this female propaganda throughout history—as Naomi Wolf, Camille Paglia, and Susan Faludi have all pointed out. For instance, women's magazines are mostly devoted to topics that make women feel paranoid that we're not thin enough, sexy enough, loving enough—just plain ol' good enough—whereas men's magazines don't bombard men with "1001 Secrets to Buffier Buns," but instead include articles about men who succeed, offering further male self-affirmation. In a way, men's magazines represent a page out of Sun Tzu's *The Art of War,* where he says:

> *"After a capture . . . replace the flags in the chariot and add them to your own force. . . . This is how you both defeat the enemy and make your own forces appear larger."*

Seeing successful men so often in movies and newspapers and magazines and on TV can be daunting to a girl's confidence, make her feel as if she's got to have a penis to get ahead.

BELLES OF THE BALLS

I find it interesting that so many famous women are eventually known in terms of their negative, not positive, attributes:

SYLVIA PLATH: SUICIDAL

JOAN OF ARC: EGOMANIACALLY CRAZED

BARBRA STREISAND: BITCHY

ROSEANNE: EVEN BITCHIER

ZELDA FITZGERALD: NUTS

FRIDA KAHLO: MUSTACHED

HILLARY CLINTON: COLD/CALCULATING

MADONNA: SLUTTY

SINEAD O'CONNOR: ANTI-POPE/
ANTIPHOTOGRAPHY

And why have bad-boy singers like Axl Rose and Snoop Doggy Dogg been forgiven by the public for their sins, but bad-girl singers like Sinead O'Connor and Madonna linger on the defendant's stand?

And while we're dissing, why are women the ones with the reputation for being "crazy bitches," when there have been zero female Mussolinis, Hitlers, and Khomeinis? (Now, those are some men who could have benefited from reading a few books on better business etiquette and stress reduction in the workplace.)

THE MEDIA:
FREEDOM OF THE SUPPRESS

J also find it interesting that here in America, land of gazillion magazines, we still have no *Working Father Magazine,* no *Family Circle for Men,* and no *Groom's Magazine* to haunt men's psyches. The results? An unmarried woman often feels a vacuum in her life, whereas an unmarried man feels maybe a small Dustbuster.

Although I've repeatedly stated that it's good to ask questions, there are three questions that are exceptions to that rule, ones I don't enjoy being asked:

1. **Why** aren't you married?
2. Why aren't **you** married?

And the ever-popular:

3. Why **aren't** you married?

Luckily I have an answer to all three out of three questions, beginning with my own question: What's so great about married people? Hitler got married. Frankenstein got married. Roseanne has even gotten married three times. Obviously married people are not superior people. However, look at some of the cool singles out there: Catwoman, Buddha, The Lone Ranger. Actually, all superheroes are single: Superman, Batman, Dudley Dooright—even the quintessential superhero: God. In fact, God runs a single-parent household. (Plus, there is no such thing as a "Stepford Single Girl.")

The problem is: Many terrific women have made themselves overqualified for the job of wife, because many men are looking for a woman with "receptionist-level wife skills," not "CEO-level wife skills." Meaning: If a woman doesn't hang on a man's every word, is too independent, challenges his leadership, wants to create her own hours, demands emotional raises, then there won't be as many openings for the kind of wife position she is seeking. One of the big problems with marriages in the nineties: no room for two husbands.

Gloria Steinem once said, "I have become the man I always wanted to marry." Well, I guess many of us women are looking to find the man who has become the wife we were supposed to be. But as many of us women have discovered, it's hard to find a guy who will make a good wife.

Basically, it's rough out there trying to juggle a relationship and a job—then throw a baby into this bathwater. Phew. Working mothers have it ultra-tough. ("Working mother." Isn't that redundant?)

Then again, *what were we women thinking?* What made us hope that we could juggle home AND work? I mean, hasn't that experiment been tried by men for all these years—with not always the most satisfying results? And career men get an extra helping of extra understanding about getting extra help at home that career women don't always get from their men.*

ANOTHER WOODY EXPLAINS THE "WOODY" PHENOMENON

*I*t seems women have been busy expanding their role in the workplace, but men haven't been nearly as busy changing their role at the homeplace. Things must change. As long as women's lives outside of work are disadvantaged in comparison to men's, women will continue to be disadvantaged at work as well.

Whose fault is it that men are not eagerly swapping roles with their wives? In many ways, it could be ours. Perhaps we women have allowed men to have their way because we're so strongly socialized to want to please. Plus, we women are not rewarded in this culture for speaking up. We're socialized to feel as if airing our grievances means we're nagging/ being demanding. Studies even show that doctors have trouble taking women's "grievances" seriously. They tend to diagnose a majority of women's symptomatic complaints as imaginary or emotionally induced with far more frequency than they diagnose men's complaints as such.

Plus, as we all know, it's difficult to try to create a change in learned thinking and behavior in *ourselves*. You can double that difficulty if you plan to create a change in learned thinking and behavior in *others*. President Woodrow Wilson agrees. In the words of Woody:

*NOTE: What I want to know is: Why can men understand all the complicated ins and outs of operating a VCR, but not an iron?

*"If you want to make enemies, try to change
something."*

And as we confirmed earlier, women in particular don't like to
make enemies.

SUPER BALLS VERSUS KICK BALLS

*S*o many voices putting doubts and negativity in your head! It takes
a lot of inner strength to tell all those voices they don't know what the
&%$#@! they're talking about.

In other words, as I've said before:

You must have balls.

And more important:

You must have the balls to keep *having balls.*

Which means—at the risk of repeating myself yet again (but hey,
after all, I am promoting risk taking):

**You must have the courage to take risks, stir up controversy, be
talked about behind your back, and talked back to by the opposition. AND until a woman can change her un-evil ways, be tough,
bear balls, face controversy, and STOP caring what people think,
then others—both men and women others—will forever have an
edge over her.**

Basically, the trick is: Do not pay too much attention to those obstacles in your way. Or . . . to quote that driven-in-every-sense-of-the-
word-driven guy, Henry Ford:

*"Obstacles are those frightful things you see
when you take your eyes off your goal."*

Remain steadfast in your decision to succeed, and you'll be just fine.

Some of you I know are probably thinking, "Yeah, right, lady. So Smarty Pants, how can this be done?"

First of all, I don't like your tone. Second of all, there are a lot of complicated answers to that question. I could write a book on it. In fact, I have. In Parts 2, 3, and 4 I'll answer this question in detail. In the meantime, here's one very simple answer. . . .

THE AARDVARK OF HAPPINESS

$\mathcal{D}$id you ever notice if someone said to you "Don't think about aardvarks," all you would think about would be aardvarks? Soon you'd notice aardvarks everywhere—even in your diet mochaccino, the way the skim milk forms little aardvark swirls in the cup. The same thing goes for happiness. If you look for it, you will always see it in things. Instead of seeing a problem, you will see an opportunity, a learning experience—a good, hearty laugh.

As I mentioned in my Introduction, I believe laughter can be an empowering aid during times of struggle. And a positive outlook is *theee* most important tool to succeed in business—next to balls. In fact, you should keep this tool right next to your balls. Basically, this means not making your ego your sole focus for feeding and nurturing, but rather prioritizing the maintenance of a balanced spirit/body/heart triumvirate.

You've got it all within you to succeed. Each and every one of us can hunt down and attain our Career Waldo. It's like this: You have all this inner potential. It's all inside you.

Actually, it's more like this: You are like one of those VCRs with the blinking 12:00, 12:00, 12:00. Sure, it's possible to stop your incessant blinking and set yourself to the proper time. In fact, if you *really* wanted, you could probably figure out how to program yourself to record seven different programs on seven different days of the week seven months in advance. Yet you don't. You've never gotten around to figuring out how to tap into all your programming options. HOWEVER, just because you don't know how to use all those options doesn't mean that you as a VCR are not capable of them.

Same goes with you as a human. You just have to take the time to discover how to tap into it all. Once you do, you can/will achieve a powerfully positive outlook—and a positively powerful and successful career. You'll probably soon discover that one follows the other. Positive attracts Positive. Just as Like attracts Like. And Love attracts Love. And Velvet attracts Cat Hair. (But that's another story.)

As the Taoists say:

> *"If we are at peace with ourselves and the*
> *world around us, success will come unsought."*

The only way to do this is to make sure that you have an earthquake-proof foundation of self-confidence and a sense of inner peace—in other words, you need the secrets and strategies in the upcoming parts.

But before I go on to those sections, I need to take two important phone calls.

TWO PHONE CALLS:

PHONE CALL #1

I was reading a J. Crew catalog while on the phone with a friend. I admit it. I am not proud. I was not fully listening. But it was a new catalog. I needed sweaters. They had mohair in periwinkle. I love mohair. I love periwinkle.

ANYWAY . . . suddenly my friend asks me, "So which of those two things do you think I should do about my office situation?"

I didn't want to admit I wasn't listening. So I paused, then said, "Do what you feel best about. You probably know in your heart."

Phew, I thought.

Then my friend said, "But I want *your* opinion. It's important to me. That's why I'm asking."

I was stuck. I knew my friend had two choices. I could gamble and say, "Do the first one." But what if I was misadvising? Then the answer came to me.

"I think," I said, "that you should do the riskier of the two things."

My friend paused, then replied, "You're right. You're absolutely right. That's what I'm going to do."

I felt good about my advice. I knew that's what I would have advised anyway, had J. Crew not been offering periwinkle mohair sweaters.

When in doubt . . .

Do the riskier thing.

PHONE CALL #2

I was on the phone with a friend at his office, and at conversation's end he said what sounded to me like "I gotta go. I hope your life has great meaning."

"What?" I asked.

"What?" he repeated.

"What did you say?" I asked again.

"I said, 'I gotta go, I'm late for this meeting.' Why?"

"Oh! I thought you said, 'I gotta go. I hope your life has great meaning.'"

We both laughed.

But if only we ended more conversations that way, huh?

Okay. Now this part is really over. I guarantee it.

Part 2

SUPPORT FOR

BALLS IN

BUSINESS

—

Slipping into
the Dressing Room
of the Heart for
a Quick Change

O ne of the good things about being a human—besides being entitled to Chinese food delivery—is that we are entitled to *consciousness*, which means we have the opportunity to think about how we can improve our lives, which not only includes taking advantage of that Chinese food delivery option, but other options, like deciding if we should change careers/change attitudes/change to MCI.

Using this consciousness perk, however, is not as easy as it should be. Often the important thing we need to be conscious of changing, we cannot see—like that ketchup bottle in the refrigerator. We're staring at it, staring at it, staring at it, but cannot find it.

The Tibetan Book of Living and Dying describes this "Ketchup Bottle in Your Face" Syndrome in a poem entitled "Autobiography in Five Chapters":

1. I walk down the street.
There is a deep hole in the sidewalk.
I fall in.
I am lost . . . I am hopeless.

It isn't my fault.
It takes forever to find a way out.

2. I walk down the same street.
There is a deep hole in the sidewalk.
I pretend I don't see it.
I fall in again.
I can't believe I'm in the same place.
But it isn't my fault.
It still takes a long time to get out.

3. I walk down the same street.
There is a deep hole in the sidewalk.
I see it is there.
I still fall in . . . it's a habit.
My eyes are open.
I know where I am.
It is my fault.
I get out immediately.

4. I walk down the same street.
There is a deep hole in the sidewalk.
I walk around it.

5. I walk down another street.

When I first read this poem, I was surprised when I got to Chapter 4 that there was a need for a Chapter 5. I remember thinking: Well, if you walk *around* the hole, isn't that the ultimate solution?

Then I read Chapter 5 and realized: Aha. *This* is exactly what I need to be doing in my career life: finding new streets—new ways to deal with those "Damn-why-didn't-I-see-it-coming career holes."

I reread the poem and saw that in the Hollywood scheme of plot development, Chapter 3 is The Big Climax. This is when one realizes one has a Habit Problem. Freud has written about this, too. He contends that we have two ways we can relive our past: (1) our memories and (2) our actions.

Many of our actions are triggered unconsciously by sheer habit. We have "knee-jerk" reactions to things—which are often "me-jerk" reactions. Change is only possible when we become conscious, as the poem states, that *"It is my fault,"* that this action is part of a "Habit Problem" —in other words, a "Pavlovian Response to Life."

In case Pavlov's name doesn't ring a bell (so to speak), let me remind you: He was the guy who rang a bell before feeding his dog, then noticed that the mere sound of the bell got Fido drooling all over his shag carpeting. I believe Good Humor trucks, with their tinkling bells, have tried to cash in on Pavlov's findings. But that's another exposé book.

In this particular book, I'd like to discuss how the sound of a ringing office phone inspires an unconscious reaction and thereby action. Unknowingly, we have trained ourselves to respond in specific and recurring ways to the various office symbols and events around us, e.g., authority figures, expense reports, large meetings, unrealistic deadlines, broken Xerox machines. Me, I usually respond by getting as hungry as a Pavlovian dog. I eat.

I've tried to find a substitute response to stress—like meditation or shoe shopping. The problem is:

Familiarity breeds "content." Newness can
breed discontent.

After all, the new street might have its share of holes. At least the holes on our regularly treaded street are the best kind: *familiar* holes. Meaning . . . the goal we should make for ourselves is to:

Discover new streets—with eyes still wide
open.

63

That is also the goal of this particular section of the book. I want to show you some new streets—but remind you to keep your eyes wide open to their holes. This is also a goal of Sun Tzu's, who reminds us:

> *"If you do not understand the harm that military actions cause, then you cannot understand the benefits to be gained through military action."*

SHOPPING IN THE BOYS' DEPARTMENT

*I*n many ways it's *logical* rather than *biological* that men have an edge over women in the workplace. They've been there longer, so they know how to find their way around the hallways of that big mall called Corporate Business.

Speaking of malls, it's now time to do some shopping.* I recommend we start in the Boys' Department, see what male attributes guys are wearing to the office. Maybe one or two are just what you need to wear to your next meeting. But before you buy into these attributes, be sure to tap into your innate shopping instincts. While reading the following male qualities, do some comparison shopping. Ask yourself: Is this male attribute well made, or will it fall apart easily? What kind of upkeep does it require? Can you afford the price you have to pay for it? Does it really, truly fit you? And IS it you? Your style?

Sun Tzu is a self-confessed big fan of comparison shopping, though that's not exactly how he put it. He put it exactly like this:

---

*Actually, it's *always* time to do some shopping. That's why God created twenty-four-hour home-shopping channels.

*"Know thyself, know thine enemy. If you under-
stand yourself, without understanding the
enemy, your chances of winning are 50/50. If
you understand neither the enemy or yourself,
you will always lose."*

With all this in mind, here's a list of "The Top Ten Male Qualities
Men Are Wearing to the Office in the Nineties" that we females should
consider wearing: "The Girls Will Be Boys Inner- and Outer-Wear
Collection." Happy shopping!

1

MEN LAST ONLY FIFTEEN
MINUTES. WOMEN CAN
GO ON FOREVER.

I'm talking about talking. I don't know where your mind was at. Anyway, my point is:

WOMEN LIKE SMALL TALK.
MEN PREFER MINUSCULE TALK.

As I mentioned in Part 1, many men in business wisely have one goal only:

Win*

Because men are better at focusing on getting the job done, they are less tempted to get sidetracked by personal stuff. They instinctively keep meetings and phone calls short.

We women, however, have a tendency to spiritedly yak, yak, yak on the phone—off on some tangent, or cosine, that doesn't help us reach our business goal.

*Preferably lots of cash and prizes.

Deborah Tannen, in her insightful books *You Just Don't Understand* and *Talking From 9 to 5,* explains why there is this difference in male/female conversational styles. According to Tannen, many women view conversations as an opportunity to emotionally connect, whereas many men view them as an opportunity to convince, instruct, and impress.

MEANING . . . Women feel very comfortable engaging in *informal* talk, whereas men feel more comfortable with *informing* talk.

Men tend to see any other kind of talk as a lavish or imprudent use of time—though, according to a recent study, men *do* think about sex about once every seven minutes, which can sure gobble up a business day, so perhaps it evens out.

What this all comes down to is very simple. One of the tricks of success is not allowing too many extravagances to consume your business day, because in today's time-scarce society:

Time = *money* + *then some.*

As you probably have noticed, we residents in the nineties have a daily list of twenty things to do, with only time to do ten—and we wind up doing thirty. We've traded in:

Quality of Life

For . . .

Quantity *of Life*

If you're anything like me, you've been picking movies and restaurants not based on desire but on *proximity*, and you don't do any activity unless you can cleave it into at least two—even ordering up Chinese food. When the delivery guy comes, I often hand him my bills and sweetly ask him to drop them in the mailbox on his way back to the Szechuan Empire. Hey, every five minutes saved helps.

But before you unplug your phone cord, keep in mind . . .

THERE'S A DISADVANTAGE
TO THIS MALE ADVANTAGE

*B*y limiting their oral pleasure, men can often miss out on the opportunity to unwind, vent, have an in-body experience, and maybe even find out about a good new Chinese food delivery opportunity. And they can miss out on a good career opportunity, because:

Short phone breaks can mean big career breaks.

For me, 50 percent of my success as a writer has been due to what I know. The other 99 percent has been due to *who* I know.*

Basically, there are four important kinds of HEALTHY phone breaks that are important to take throughout a business day:

The Four Basic Office Phone Call Groups:

1. Specific information exchange
2. Pep talks
3. Advice
4. Gossip

Surprisingly enough, sharing gossip is strongly recommended by Sun Tzu, who says:

> *"You must look to reports of reliable spies*
> *before you will understand the circumstances*
> *of the enemy."*

Occasional frivolous yakking can even lead to higher productivity. Ironically, it is often when one stops thinking about a career problem that one starts solving that issue. That's why some of our best ideas come to us in the bathroom.**

*NOTE: That was *not* bad math. Believe me, that equation adds up.

**NOTE: Perhaps one of the secrets to success is to eat lots of prunes and bran muffins . . . ?

Finally, keep in mind that:

*Breaks now
are better than
breakdowns later.*

And speaking of breaks, it's time for an exercise break. . . .

Staremaster
For Improved Conversational Tactics

1. The book *What They Don't Teach You at Harvard Business School* suggests trying to be the initiator of phone calls, not the receiver. It helps you keep focused and thereby shortens calls. Sun Tzu also recommended this when he said:

   "Whoever arrives at the battlefield first will be at ease and in a position to take the initiative."

   (Interestingly, this philosophy also explains how macrocosmically, in the grand scheme of business, men have an edge over women. They arrived FIRST on the corporate battlefield. We're on their turf.)
2. *What They Don't Teach You at Harvard Business School* also suggests that if you must take an incoming call, pause before picking up the receiver and ask yourself what ONE goal do you want to accomplish by conversation's end.
3. Know your own work habits. Determine which are your best hours for doing the hardest part of your job, and avoid calls during this time. Save phone time for downtime, not prime time. For instance, some people are morning people. Others are end-of-the-day people. Me, I'm a 3:00 P.M. to 3:05 P.M. person. That's my best time.
4. If you have a really torturous day, use the phone as a self-bribe.

Tell yourself: One call for the office, one call for me.

5. Although gossip has Sun Tzu's celebrity endorsement, remember:

Gossip is better to receive than to give.

Spreading gossip can be both logically bad for your image and spiritually bad for karma. Most important, don't gossip about yourself. Avoid talking about your sex life to coworkers. It will tarnish your professionalism. They don't need to hear about the latest man you're sleeping with—unless, of course, it's John F. Kennedy, Jr. Then, by all means, tell EVERYBODY.*

6. I recommend women try on a size fifteen-minute phone call. If need be, alert the listener from the start that you have to be somewhere by a certain time—invent a meeting. And although I do not recommend faking orgasm, I do recommend faking call waiting to get off the phone. Multiple call waiting if you must.

7. Try always to be the one who ends the conversation. This is a subliminal power edge.

8. Avoid phone tag. Notice what time people usually call you. Most people have a pattern. Call people at these times. Or ask them directly what times are good. Make phone appointments. Another good tip: If you need permission from someone for something, leave a message asking for that something, and say that if you *don't* hear back, then you'll assume no news is affirmative news.

9. Be especially aware of what people reveal toward the close of conversations. This relaxed phase is when they will be most honest and real.

*NOTE: Why is it that men do *not* want to hear about other men a woman has slept with, but are open to hearing about all the *women* a woman has slept with? Go figure.

10. If you sense that the other person has to go, then GO. Don't waste people's time.

11. Avoid calls from people who are downers—or what I call "Red Sweater/Green Sweater People," from a joke I once heard. A woman gives her nephew two sweaters, a red one and a green one. When she later visits him, he's wearing the red sweater, and she says, "What's the matter? You don't like the green sweater?" Red sweater/green sweater people can drain you of energy—and energy is the fuel for success.

12. Be aware of what should be talked about on the phone versus in person. Remember: The medium is the message. And calls should be a small medium. If a topic requires more than thirty minutes, or is highly important, consider setting up a 3-D appointment. Calls lack the added benefit of eye contact and body language and flaky almond croissants. Too often in the nineties, we deal with plastic phones, not-in-the-flesh people, and we miss out. There's a new hipster expression called "Skintime," meaning time spent in person with other persons—a growing rarity.

2

REPRESSION IS BETTER
THAN DEPRESSION

*M*any men, being more warrior than worrier, feel a certain way about making mistakes. They don't feel. They move on. They instinctively know what Ayn Rand knows—which is what a coal miner knows:

> *"[He] knows that it's not his feelings that keep
> the coal carts moving under the earth—and he
> knows what does keep them moving."*

Getting upset about something won't help but hinder. To illustrate, there's a Taoist fable:

> *A man was walking in the desert. Suddenly he
> was bitten by a poisonous snake. He became so
> obsessed with fear and worry about the poison
> that he forgot to take action to suck out the
> poison. He died. The end.*

Baltasar Gracián, author of *The Art of Worldly Wisdom*, warns against this downward-spiral propensity:

"Don't turn one act of foolishness into two.
One lie leads to another greater one and it is
the same with folly."

The same way like attracts like, negativity attracts negativity. Depression is an energy drainer that exhausts our ability to move forward.

Sometimes there's nothing you can do about a situation, except tell yourself: Everything happens for a reason. Usually that reason is: My boss is an asshole. But move on. There's no reason to live in the past. You're supposed to be living here in the present. Remember? What do you need to live in two places for? Gracián advises:

"Know how to forget. Not only does memory
behave basely, not coming forward when it is
needed, it is also foolish, for it comes to us
when it shouldn't. It is prolix when it can give
us pain, and careless when it can give us plea-
sure. Let us train the memory and teach it
better manners."

While we're at it, let us also train our memory to know what the heck that word *prolix* means. I keep forgetting. Ready? I looked it up for us.

pro-lix, *(pro-liks); adj, long, drawn out;*
diffuse; wordy. –ly adv, –ity n. (L. prolixus)

There's also a prolixity of beauty articles starring women in their you-could-be-prettier faces, which make women angst-ridden, and drain off positive energy resources needed to achieve goals—as Naomi Wolf has brought to our attention. These self-loathing emotions should most definitely be repressed. As I mentioned in Part 1, to reach our goals, we women need to learn to be warriors, not worriers. We need to retrain ourselves to see the Aardvark of Happiness where we think we are only seeing Porcupines of Pain. Unfortunately, it's hard to see the difference between an aardvark and a porcupine when your vision is so clouded up with negativity.

Chances are you've noticed that "hindsight" usually comes with twenty-twenty vision, and that it's highly appropriate that the word has that prefix "hind" in it because we usually feel like one of those—a horse's one of those—when we look back at situations.

The reason we are finally able to view things clearly with hindsight is simple: The static of our emotions is no longer fuzzying up our view. We no longer have emotions at stake because what's past is past. When this emotional static finally settles down, it's like getting cable hookup to a situation that used to be without cable hookup. Not only is the picture clearer, but you also have more viewing options. This is what William Blake was referring to when he wrote:

"If the doors of perception were cleansed every-thing would appear to man as it is, infinite."

We women need to work on getting twenty-four-hour-a-day emotional cable hookup—BUT HERE'S THE CATCH. We have to learn how to tune into this emotional cable hookup WHILE a tense situation is in action, instead of three years later—or even three months later. Even three days later is three days of wasted time and emotions that can bog down a career.

There are two ways to get better emotional cable hookup:

1. Medicate
2. Meditate

I recommend the latter. I know there are a lot of wonderful and helpful mood medications on the market, but I believe the mind and body are in cahoots, and if we work at calming the mind, our stress level will go down, which in turn will help calm our mind, which in turn will ease stress, ad infinitum—even in ad agency infinitum.

Coming up soon in the Staremaster section, I'll be giving a helpful sample meditation, but there are many activities—exercise, writing in your journal, baking bread—that can serve the same function as meditation. Still, meditation itself is the most mediative of them all—plus it has the advantage of being more easily done at the office than, say, baking a loaf of rye bread.

But before you try to machine-gun down all the Porcupines of Pain in view, consider . . .

THERE ARE DISADVANTAGES TO THIS MALE ADVANTAGE

*D*ealing with depression with repression also means less opportunity for evolving—and a potential serial killer hobby. As Jung said:

> *"When an inner situation is not made*
> *conscious, it appears outside as fate."*

This fate can be anything from a car crash to lost office keys to the flu to a serial killer hobby. All of these are attempts by our subconscious to get us to face up to our depression—become self-aware—and porcupine aware. Without this awareness . . .

I'm having one of those days

can easily turn into . . .

I'm having one of those years.

The subconscious knows this and works hard to get us to perk up and change—so hard it never even goes to sleep. It works all through the night, even in our dreams—especially in our dreams. The subconscious should actually receive bigger and better billing than mere "sub" status. It should be called our "above"-conscious, because it makes more of our life decisions than our conscious. It's in charge of how many sick days we get, how messy our home is—even how messy our love life is. It's also the reason why our diaries often look like Madlibs. For instance:

> **Dear Diary,**
> I'm _____ *(mad, resentful, depressed)* **that**
> _____ *(my boyfriend, boss, mother)* **doesn't** _____
> *(listen to me, respect me, love me more)*. **It reminds me of what**
> **happened** _____ *(last week, last month, last year, next*
> *week, next month, next year)* **with** _____ *(my boyfriend, my*
> *boss, my mother)*. **I swear to** _____ *(God, Buddha, my ther-*
> *apist, my manicurist)* **I won't let this happen again!**

Our subconscious is hoping that all of our repeated patterns will eventually piss us off enough to get us to want to change, will make us "sick and tired" of how things are going in every sense of those words, meaning we can physically find ourselves "sick and tired." The Taoists call this a "kriya," a "spiritual tantrum" that leads to finally becoming determined to change and start filling in those blanks of our diaries with cheerier adjectives, more positive verbs.

For example, you may find yourself saying:

My boss is pushing my buttons.

These buttons are your potential kriyas, places inside you where you have major potential for growth. So don't think of it as:

My boss is pushing my buttons.

Think of it as . . .

My boss is pushing my growth opportunity.

As Aldous Huxley said:

"Experience is not what happens to a man, it is what a man does with what happens to him."

The problem is it's painful to undergo a kriya, although in the long run, it's for the best—similar to how an operation might be for our best, but we'd rather put it off, ignore its pressing need. In the end, the operation can make you healthier—though sometimes it can also make you dead. But as they say . . .

"What doesn't kill you makes you stronger— and gives you good screenplay material."

Or as the Chinese doctors say:

One disease, long life; no disease, short life.

The trick is not to repress to the negative stuff that can hurt us big-time in the long run and repress the negative stuff that hurts our opportunity to succeed in what we're doing in the present. The trick to this trick is to know how to tell the difference between these two—and thereby pick the right things to repress and not to repress in our lives.

Thomas Edison knew how to do this—which made him not only smart, but wise. He started off his career by blowing up his laboratory. His employer told him he'd never amount to anything. He could have gotten depressed, but instead he got repressed. Rather than indulge in a bad mood that blowing up a laboratory can put a guy in, he moved forward. Today he is considered one of the foremost inventors in American history.

All successful people have mastered the art of knowing when and what to repress. Like Walt Disney. He was fired by a newspaper editor for lack of ideas and went bankrupt several times before Disneyland was built. Henry Ford went bankrupt *five* times. Chances are all the folks in the Fortune 500 could just as easily be members of the Misfortune 500. Which reminds me of one of my favorite Taoist fables:

Having a Cow over a Cow

There was this father and son who had a black cow that one day gave birth to a white calf. They asked the kingdom's wise man what this meant, and were told it was a sign of great fortune. A week later the father went blind in one eye. A bunch of months after that, the black cow again gave birth to a white calf. The one-eyed father told his son to ask the wise man yet again what this meant. The son refused, insisting that this wise man was a wise guy, an obvious quack, since his father had experienced such bad fortune. The father insisted, so begrudgingly the son went. The wise man again foresaw good fortune. A week later, the son went blind in both eyes. As if that was not bad enough, a few weeks after that their kingdom got into a big fight with another kingdom. War ensued. All the able-bodied, able-sighted men went to battle. Most of them died. But the father and son, who were not fit for war, were spared. It was then that the son realized that misfortune can, in time, become fortune. And it was then that the son and his father got their sight back.

Time is a mysterious, restorative, and, for the most part, kind-natured force. It heals. And when it doesn't heal, it at least reveals. We must trust that there is a lesson to be learned from the constant ebb and flow in this universe. (And usually when I'm "flowing," I'm ebbing, if you know what I mean. But that's another story, and not a very Taoist one.)

Staremaster
For Dealing Better with Depression

1. The next time you feel your career is over FOREVER, repeat the following mantra: John Travolta is back, John Travolta is back, John Travolta is back, John Travolta is back, John Travolta is back, John Travolta is back, John Travolta is back, John Travolta is back, John Travolta is back, etc. . . .

2. Two singers sang it well. Edith Piaf sang it first in French: "Je ne regrette rien. J'avance," which, translated, means "I regret nothing. I move forward." Alanis Morissette sang it next in English: "You cry you learn, you lose you learn." Both songs translate out the same: Always try to focus on finding the hidden lesson in the lessening of your happiness.

3. If you'd like to learn the art of repression, you can start by learning under a "Substitute Teacher." Every time a depressing thought enters your mind, substitute it with a positive one that will teach you to think positively about life. If you look for it, every day something good _does_ happen. For instance, today you learned once and for all what the word _prolix_ means. Chances are things are always better in your life on second glance. Keep in mind what Colette, the writer, said:

   "What a wonderful life I've had.
   I only wish I'd realized it sooner."

4. A relationship counselor once told me he can predict the success of a couple _not_ by how well they got along, but by how well they _didn't_ get along. A couple was only as good as their worst

moment. How did they handle conflict? He believed there were three possibilities:

a. Fighting—not listening to each other because you're both busy arguing your points.
b. Avoidance—neither of you want to talk about it.
c. Validation—both of you listen to each other, validate each other's point of view, and try to reconcile.

Number three was the number-one solution. I thought about how this was not only true for love relationships but *all* relationships, including with bosses—and even our internal selves. How do we deal with our internal conflicts? Do we avoid looking at them? If so, this is repression—and we should check out some of that validation stuff when appropriate. How can you tell appropriate repression from inappropriate repression? As I mentioned, meditation makes a good emotional cable hookup. Let me thereby hook you up with the following:

Try to find a quiet time and place. (I know: Yeah, right!) Sit upright, with legs crossed in the lotus position, right hand on right knee, left hand on left knee. Close your eyes. Become aware of your spine. Ease the tension in it. Become aware of your neck. Ease the tension there. Do the same for: feet, legs, buns, tummy. Notice what sounds you hear, what thoughts you think. As each thought comes up, name it "my past" or "my future." Try to get into the present. Say to yourself: "I am here now." Breathe deeply. Become aware of your breath—its in-and-out motion. Breathe very deeply for ten breaths. Repeat less deeply for another ten. Try to do this for at least ten minutes. When you stop, do so slowly. Do not jolt up and go back to work.

3

AGGRESSION IS BETTER THAN DEPRESSION/ REPRESSION

*M*any screwed-over businessmen have a helpful philosophy:

Despise others, instead of oneself.

This leads to perkier moods, a reservoir of feral energy that can be channeled into demigod work abilities, and the desire to crush beer cans with one's head.

Many of us women, however, feel guilty about responding to office conflicts with aggression and anger. We are socialized to internalize negative emotions rather than externalize them.

The results of our differences?

1. Women commit suicide—or get committed.
2. Men commit homicide—or get raises.

Women can benefit from learning to rechannel anger—and many are starting to. Behind many a successful woman is a man who pissed her off: e.g., Ivana Trump.

If you have trouble acknowledging your anger, remember that holding it in:

1. Uses up a lot of energy
2. Potentially won't get you more respect but LESS

Baltasar Gracián says:

> *"Don't be bad by being too good. You will be if you never get angry. . . . Sweetness alone is for children and fools."*

Another problem women face is falling prey to becoming second-degree martyrs by believing they are speaking up when really they are speaking sideways, in an indirect way that is hard to fully understand. Then later these women get miffed when men can't read their minds. Which reminds me of . . .

A Deaf Story About a Blind Date

My buddy David told me he wanted to fix me up with his friend. After he got done describing his friend, I asked David how he had described me to him.

"I told him you were a victim," David said.

I knew I must have heard David wrong.

"What did you say?" I asked.

"I said you were a vixen," David repeated.

"Why, is that bad?"

"No, no, not at all," I said, relieved.

So remember:

VIXEN, GOOD.

VICTIM, BAD.

There's a lot of benefit to being in touch with your anger— even anger you don't ultimately decide to express verbally, because often this is what it takes to bring things to full consciousness, full clarity. Some of the best periods in my life have been what I call my:

Post–"fuck this" periods

Sometimes you have to reach:

Fuck this!!!!!!!!!

to be motivated to get to

Post–"fuck this."

Many post–"fuck this" periods fall under the category of "kriyas" and are a fertile time for self-transformation, full of multiple epiphanies —and life-changing career moves. As Sogyal Rinpoche, author of *The Tibetan Book of Living and Dying,* explains:

> *"When you fall from a great height, there is only one possible place to land: on the ground —the ground of truth. . . . Falling is in no way a disaster, but the discovery of an inner refuge."*

Or as the popular expression goes: It's always darkest before the dawn. Thanks to my career in advertising, I've even had the chance to research this expression because I was often up till dawn working, and let me tell you, it *does* get pretty dark right before dawn hits.

My point is: Dawn eventually does come. And when it does, things get illuminated. Hence the expression "it dawned on someone."

However, before you get mad as hell and #$%@! aren't gonna take it anymore, consider . . .

THERE ARE DISADVANTAGES TO THIS MALE ADVANTAGE

*M*any men can be too in touch with their anger, and can thereby become:

Cross stressers

Meaning, they can find themselves . . .

Burning the bridge at both ends.

Or to put it yet another way:

Having a penis makes some men feel they have a license to be a dick.

A savvy woman can use a man's bad temper to her advantage. As Sun Tzu advises:

"When they are angry, perturb them."

T'ai chi martial-arts masters back him up, by suggesting:

"Use your enemies' strength against him."

If/when you do get a man to start screaming, know that you have won the argument. Similarly, keep in mind if/when YOU start screaming, know that YOU have lost the argument.

Remember that relationship counselor who listed those three possibilities for dealing with conflict? Once again, they were:

1. Fighting
2. Avoidance
3. Validation

Number three still remains number one. Taoists have many sound bites that back this up. They say:

*"Strength will break, where weakness will
remain intact."*

and

"To bend is to stay whole"

ALSO . . . keep in mind that, ironically, stern directives often communicate WEAKNESS, not power. For example, you know how someone who doesn't know how to make a lawnmower work will kick it? That's what many of these angry aggressive types are doing, responding to a person whom they don't understand, and whom they feel powerless around, with the same resolve they do with that lawnmower: If I kick it, then it will work.

A person who bellows commands is often foolishly caught up in his title and the ego gratification authority brings, or is a graduate of the "Me Think Thou Dost Protest Too Much School of Insecurity." Either way they're acting—or rather *overacting*—out of ego. And as we know . . .

*The ego bone is connected to the Achilles heel
bone.*

The trick is remembering: You should not be afraid of someone's abusive directives, especially if you can figure out what their Achilles heel is. Even if you can't, remain secure in the knowledge that these folks who bellow boldly want you to fear them, because they fear you won't listen to them otherwise—due to ego-gone-awry insecurity.

The good news is: Many of these angry folks yell before they think, operating under the philosophy:

I'll burn down that bridge when I get to it.

MEANING . . . Their communication style won't serve them well in the long run, because . . .

Where there's smoke, you get fired.

When office power changes, these people are often the first to go.

Plus, often this type of reflex anger can cloud over the clarity of a situation. Buddha has a theory on anger and aggression: "Learn to respond, not to react." This entails:

1. Making a choice NOT to be angry.
2. Making a choice to FAKE being angry.

So if you find yourself tempted to express your anger verbally, REMEMBER, it's best to wait until the smoke of your internal fires fade, before you act with aggression—and best always to be merely acting in the Meryl Streep sense of the word *act*. (Though be careful not to *over-act* the part in the grade B actor/director Ed Wood's sense of the word.) The goal when dealing with upsetting situations should be to strike a balance (without striking any secretaries) of the following:

1. Don't give a fuck what people think about your aggression.
2. Don't fuck over anybody.
3. Get out of it all—and still remain fuckable later that night.

$\mathcal{S}$taremaster
For Dealing with Aggression

1. Make no decisions when you are angry. Wait to speak until after you've counted "one hundred fuck you's"—or until PMS passes*—whichever comes first. And remember:

---

*Which reminds me: Why does everyone believe in the reality of a man's testosterone-induced misbehavior, but a woman's PMS is still the UFO of body chemistry? Why do women have a reputation for being overly emotional, when it's men who respond to stress by stabbing, shooting, slicing, and dicing? Why do men get so grossed out by even the mere mention of a woman's menstrual cycle, yet love watching gory films about stabbing, shooting, slicing, and dicing? Why? XY is why, if you know what I mean.

   a. No screaming at the office.

   b. No crying either.

2. You can vent your anger on the phone by yelling—BUT while the mute button is pressed down.

3. There is only ONE excuse for getting truly angry: when you're having (grumble, grumble) computer problems. Remember "The Twinkie Defense" a few years back that got that guy off of a double-murder charge? Well, I predict a Computer Problem Defense *very shortly.* Any jury member with a computer would *have* to compassionately let the guy go.

4. Remember: Acquiring equal rights should not include equal rights to be a jerk.

4

SPORTS LESSONS

*O*ne reason men have an edge in business is because they learn helpful lessons from sports—consciously and subconsciously. Some of the general sports lessons men learn are: how to deal with competition, how to be part of a team interaction, how to lose well and win well— and that bravura and hype will only get a player so far. At the end of a game, you can find out objectively how good a player is by how many touchdowns he's made. There's nothing subjective about winning. A winner is a person who wins. Some of the lessons men learn from specific sports:

BASKETBALL

*I*n the acclaimed documentary *Hoop Dreams*, one coach explains what's needed to get into the NBA. It's not enough to have talent and passion, he says. You need to be unafraid of taking shots from the outside. Same goes for making the NBA equivalency of all careers.

BASEBALL

*B*abe Ruth was not only the highest hitter of home runs but the highest at striking out—because he took risks. We babes can learn from this Babe. Plus, as Casey Stengel said, "Good pitching will always stop good hitting and vice versa."

SKIING

*T*hey say you haven't really learned to ski until you've gotten snow on you. Same applies to slip-ups and falling on your face at the office. Plus, many Olympic skiers visualize going down the mountain smoothly/speedily every morning, before they even get on the mountain.

TENNIS

*B*illie Jean King wisely stated that in tennis, "never confuse movement for action." Same goes with work at the office. Plus, a known tennis tip for improving one's game is: Play with a better opponent. Same goes with who you should surround yourself with at the office.

ARCHERY

*T*here's a famous quote in *Zen and the Art of Archery:* "Fundamentally the marksman aims at himself." Same applies with what one aims for at work.

BOXING

*I*n *Raging Bull*, boxer Jake La Motta's manager brother got him psyched to risk entering the fight with the rousing reminder: "If you win, you win. And if you lose, you win."

T'AI CHI

*T*he first thing a new student is taught is not how to hit but how to fall, because if you're not afraid of falling, you can take more risks.

ROWING

*T*he trick to getting the farthest fastest on a lake is not with a lot of energy put into a lot of short strokes, but with a lot of power put into fewer and longer strokes. Same goes with one's work—and how many assignments one should take on.

LONG-DISTANCE RUNNING

*F*irst of all: Pace yourself. Second of all: Believe in the impossible. There's an amusing recurring pattern in marathon racing. Once an impossible marathon record is broken, suddenly other runners are also able to break this "impossible" record—because that impossible speed suddenly seems possible.

SHORT-DISTANCE RUNNING

The most important part of the race is *before* the race. You must mentally prepare yourself to take off the moment the gun goes off.

SWIMMING

Gracián offered a great swimmer's-ed tip: "It is when you are drowning that you learn to swim."

FOOTBALL

If you want to have a great fast-running quarterback, you need to have a strong center. Everything depends on the center.

GOLF

As they say: "Different strokes for different folks—and different holes." As Arnold Palmer says: "Don't get too self-satisfied or you'll lose your edge."

POKER

Poker has lots in common with business, such as: You must know when to cut losses, when to bluff, and how to use intimidation. You must be aware not only of the cards you are holding but also the cards *others might be holding*, where they are at in the game.

But before you start making those raw-egg and wheat germ vitamin B-12 protein shakes, consider . . .

THERE ARE DISADVANTAGES TO THIS MALE ADVANTAGE

*U*ou can twist an ankle doing some of those crazy sports. Meanwhile, nobody ever hurt themselves opening a box of Entenmann's Banana Crunch Loaf.*

Another disadvantage: Sports can be a major distraction from other more important life issues. Many men spend more time working out and improving their body—their outer shell—than their inner spirit and soul.**

Staremaster
For Sportmeisters

1. Climb up on one of those real Stairmasters for twenty minutes, at least three times a week—and preferably in the mornings, to get your day "trajectory-ing" off to a good start. It will help

---

*What I want to know is: Why do so many men love showing off their bravery—risking their lives and assorted body parts in inane athletic stunts—then, when the time comes to risking a little commitment, say to a woman, say to a woman they're even living with, they can become suddenly fearful? Go figure.

**Another thing I want to know: Why are women made fun of for following soap operas, yet men aren't teased for following its sweatier equivalent, sports? Oh, and while I'm popping these sports questions out of left field, I ask: Why can men remember esoteric dates of great moments in sports history but forget the dates of a live-in loved one's birthday or anniversary?

release work stress. And keep you in good general health. And remember, the mind and body are one.

2. Learn Knicks 101—or whatever sport your male office mates are into. Memorize a few key conversational start-ups, like "That Starkey sure needs to make more shots from the outside, huh?" I have no idea what I said, but some male coworker in some office somewhere does, and that's what matters in the most important game of all: Corporate Life.

3. Sneak into the boys' room: Play a sport with the boys, like golf or squash. It will not only help you Boy Network but also help you understand "Boy Psychology" and metaphorically reveal a lot about your own strengths and weaknesses in the workplace.*

*NOTE: Be sure to schedule a massage appointment for the next day.

94

5

GUILTY UNTIL
PROVEN INNOCENT

*M*en are less trusting and more paranoid than women, which are helpful Darwinian survival skills for the corporate world. The old Karen, which is really the young Karen, versus the new Karen, which is the old Karen—if you know what I mean—ANYWAY, the old young Karen used to believe everything that everyone in business told me (or rather *her*). Even (embarrassingly enough) L.A. film producers and agents—as I confessed earlier in my Introduction. The old young Karen even actually thought these people were "friends."

> THEY SOUNDED LIKE FRIENDS.
> THEY SMILED LIKE FRIENDS.
> THEY LAUGHED LIKE FRIENDS.
> THEY DINED LIKE FRIENDS.
> THEY HUGGED LIKE FRIENDS.
> THEY JUST PLAIN SMELLED LIKE FRIENDS.

HOWEVER, when the time came to negotiate contracts, the smell they emitted changed—in a bad way. (I'd rather not get into it. Just insert here a story wherein these "friends" morphed into sneaky, poisonous snakes.)

Oddly enough, at the time, I was glad I had originally chosen to trust these people. I thought:

Trusting = my optimism about people's nature.

Now I realize . . .

Trusting = my naïveté.

Amazing, huh, that I could still be naive having graduated from the School of Hard Knocks: the advertising business? Considering my time spent in the ad biz, I'd have thought I would have learned that important lesson: "Some People Lie." I'm *still* amazed every time I drink a glass of water and it doesn't spurt out the knife holes in my back. Unfortunately, the ad biz had merely given me a B.S. in b.s. One needs a full-fledged master's degree to deal with the folks in the L.A. film business—or any business in which the potential money verges on stupendous.

The new Karen knows better:

A person in business who has money at stake
that revolves around you = not a friend.

That's a person who understands that success means:

Socialize

Sometimes it even means:

Social lies

I'm not the first woman to go on a tour of Gullible's Travels. As I said, women tend to be more trusting than men. Really. Trust me on this. Not that I'm a *prude* about lies. I accept the fact that some serve a positive purpose. For instance, there's an inherent kindness in:

WE LOVE YOUR IDEA.
HE'S IN A MEETING.

IF ONLY WE HAD AN OPENING, WE'D HIRE YOU.
NO, REALLY, I DO LOVE YOUR NEW HAIRCUT.

These bent truths are similar to those found in romance—and are *usually* kosher. Admittedly, words are not *always* best used to communicate true concepts, but to miscommunicate to save feelings. Gracián supports occasional bent truths:

> *"Don't lie, but don't tell the whole truth.*
> *Nothing requires more skill than the truth,*
> *which is like letting blood from the heart. It*
> *takes skill to both speak it and withhold it. . . .*
> *Not all truths can be spoken—some should be*
> *silenced for your own sake, others for the sake*
> *of someone else."*

However, just like in romance, some truths are meant to remain both unbendable—and nonbreakable. *If we are not aware of this,* when we open up a box of these truths and discover them broken, shattered, in shards, we are in danger of becoming broken, shattered, in shards. *These* damaged truths are not inspired by kindness, but the selfish need to reach an end goal at any cost. The Truth Mutilator rationalizes:

My ends justify my mean-spirited means.

Because this single-goal focus is something men have mast—

(No. I can't say it. But, hey, this *is* a book that's meant to get us all thinking, right? With that in mind, I'll blurt ahead.)

Because this single-goal focus is something men have mastered better than women, it might follow that more men than women could find themselves motivated to tell a broken truth to get what they want. *And* because a person who fibs is ALSO a person who suspects others of fibbing, this might be why more men than women are so suspicious of others' motives.

BUT before you decide to Wite-Out all your business associates from your Christmas card list, consider . . .

THERE ARE DISADVANTAGES TO THIS MALE ADVANTAGE

*T*oo much distrust can paralyze, cut off the circulation of warm blood to your heart, which is necessary if you're to move forward in a business deal. If you never trust anyone, you'll always be looking for trouble, and maybe even create it in the process. People will be insulted by your lack of faith. Or they'll sense your discomfort and question YOUR motives.

Distrust can boomerang right back at you. Or worse, eventually, distrust can spread like that horrific virus in the movie *Outbreak*—or like it does in that town called L.A. It can create a businessperson who mistakenly winds up learning the lesson:

trust all people less

instead of merely learning . . .

trust less people.

Which reminds me of a conversation I had with my L.A. agent:

L.A. Agent: The film studio said they'd *definitely* get back to us by the end of the week.
Me: Translation, please?
L.A. Agent: What?
Me: Does "end of the week" mean "end of the month" or "end of the deal," or does it actually mean "end of the week"? You see, since last year, my new motto is "Everybody lies to me. Trust no one."

L.A. Agent: Well, your motto's just not accurate.

Me(shocked): No?

L.A. Agent: No, it should be "Everybody lies to everybody."

What this meant was: I should keep an extra-watchful eye on this agent. Since this agent thinks everybody lies to everybody, that gives *him* permission to lie since this is how he believes the business world operates. He's rationalized permission to lie.

This is what too much distrust can do to a guy—or a gal: transform them into a person who no longer sees lies as lies, but as part of an ordinary, run-of-the mill business day (which is yet another lie in progress). It is a lie a person tells himself to rationalize his need to lie.

I believe some of the worst lies told in business are the ones we tell ourselves. This includes everything from:

> *Lying is part of a business day. So it's okay if I*
> *tell a lie.*

>   to

> *I promise myself that this will be my last lie.*

>   to

> *I promise myself that as soon as I finish this*
> *report, I will quit my job and pursue becoming*
> *the next Quentin Tarantino.*

>   to

> *I promise myself I will finish this chapter that*
> *I'm now writing and have it ready for Sherri*
> *(my editor) by Monday morning.*

The problem is: If we start off lying to ourselves, and repeat these internal lies out loud, we will, without meaning to, lie to others. In so doing, we become low-grade pathological liars, because we are truly believing the white lies we tell ourselves to be Technicolored truths. You won't even realize you've told a lie—until the chapter you promised on

Monday is NOT ready on Monday. Then you realize—at the same time as your editor—that . . .

Oooops. I lied.

(NOTE: Sorry, Sherri. I really did think this chapter would be ready on Monday.)

In the end, your editor or boss or associate or whoever might wind up questioning your veracity capacity from thereon ever after.

So . . . You need to start your "Let's Be Honest Program" with *yourself.* You must learn to be honest with yourself BEFORE you open your mouth to talk.

Meaning . . .

If you want to walk your talk, don't try to run your talk.

Meaning . . .

You have to first have a talk with your ego.

It's usually an overactive ego that gets you into these messes. An overactive ego results in:

PRIDE,
which leads to
not wanting to admit weakness or failing
which can lead to:
THE NEED TO LIE

or

OVERCONFIDENCE,
which leads to
not wanting to face up to the difficulties of the
work ahead,
which can lead to
THE NEED TO LIE

or

CONSTANT NEED FOR LOVE AND
APPROVAL,
which leads to
the desire to show off or say what others want
to hear,
which can lead to
THE NEED TO LIE

I'll be discussing how to deal with a bratty ego in an upcoming chapter, but first . . .

Staremaster
For Truth-Telling/Sensing Skills

1. Success means *assess*. If you plan to go into business with someone, get to know him well first. Watch how he treats co-workers, his spouse, waitresses in restaurants, his dog. If he's manipulative or dishonest with them, he could be with you.
2. Before you get lured into telling a lie, remember: A single lie can go on your permanent record, tarnish your reputation permanently.
3. Some tips that body-language experts say might reveal that someone is lying:
   a. He scratches his nose as he talks.
   b. She looks upward and rightward as she talks.
   c. He can't look you right in the eye.
   d. She has her fingers crossed behind her back.
4. Trust your first impressions about a person—BUT be open to his or her making a second impression on you.
5. If huge gobs and gobs of money are at stake, take whatever the

people involved tell you, divide by 2, and subtract 20. (In L.A., divide by 7 and subtract 120.)

6. Never, ever, ever, EVER lie on a résumé—or anything tangible, touchable, listenable, or seeable, like a memo, a written report, or an answering machine message.

6

THE BEST THINGS IN
LIFE ARE ME

*M*ost men can teach most women the lesson of self-fulfilling confidence. It works like magic—or a good chain letter. If you believe great fortune is in the making, it is. If you believe there will be a curse upon you and your dog, then I don't recommend you and your poochie go for a late-night stroll together.

You become your expectations. Eventually your internal thoughts manifest themselves externally. It's the old "so within, so without" thingie—which is actually the principle behind "the rich get richer" thingie. The rich already view themselves as rich (their internal sense), so they are better able to bring more riches to themselves (the external manifestation). So, if in the end we get what we expect, then it makes sense that from the start we should expect some pretty damn good stuff.

People with low self-esteem (or would that be "elf"-esteem if it's low?) limit their expectations. The result? You can become your own worst enemy—potentially even more of an enemy to yourself than that competitive viper coworker down the hall.

A Cool Metaphor from Deepak Chopra

Deepak Chopra tells a story about fish who grew up in an aquarium with a glass wall down the middle that blocked them from swimming to the other side. Later, when the glass wall was removed, these fish still never swam to the other side. They limited themselves to swimming in the same confined area they'd grown accustomed to.

For me, this brings to mind how many females who grew up socialized to limit their expectations are now dealing with the business world. Some part of them feels safe remaining in a restricted success zone, because they only have a limited vision of success as they go up the corporate ladder. They can't see that the ladder does indeed go higher and higher, if they'd only just keep climbing.

A Cool Story from My Dad

My dad swears this story is true. It was his first time ever sailing. He'd just had a lovely day, and was sailing back to port, when he saw a man waving frantically at him from the dock. My dad didn't have any idea why the guy looked so frenzied. When my dad disembarked, the guy rushed over and explained. He'd been trying to stop my dad from bringing the boat in at that 180-degree angle. Sailboats just canNOT do that sort of thing. BUT that IS how my dad had ultimately brought in his boat—at that impossible angle. Because my dad did not know he couldn't, *he* could.

In Buddhism, this is called "beginner's mind"—when one can see and do more, by knowing less. "Beginner's mind" helps in brainstorming and all new business ventures. When I quit my job in advertising to become a novelist, I had "beginner's mind," because I wasn't being entirely realistic about how impossible it is to get published. On the other hand, my boyfriend at that time thought that I had gone "out of my mind" quitting to write a novel. He was a red sweater/green sweater guy.

"Do you know how DIFFICULT it is to sell a novel?" he said. "Don't get your hopes up. You'd be better off thinking you *won't* be published, so you won't be disappointed."

"What?" I said. "That makes no sense. Did Rocky go into the fight thinking, 'Hey, I might not win'?"

Our poor egos. They have to put up with a lot of naysayers. Just remember, though, that there are 4 billion people in this world, and nearly that many opinions. What's one measly opinion in the grand scheme of 4 billion? Your ego should be strong enough to withstand a one-billionth worldview of you. BUT . . . that's just *my* measly one-billionth opinion. Here's another—from Teddy Roosevelt, who said:

> *"It is not the critic who counts, not the man who points out how the strong man stumbles or where the doer of deeds could have done them better. The credit belongs to the man who is actually in the arena, whose face is marred by dust and sweat and blood, who strives valiantly, who errs and comes up short again and again because there is no effort without error and shortcomings, who knows the great devotion, who spends himself in a worthy cause, who at best knows in the end, the high achievement of triumph and who at worst, if he fails while daring greatly, knows his place*

shall never be with those timid and cold souls
who know neither victory nor defeat."

Another Roosevelt—Eleanor—had a good outlook on critics, too. She said:

"No one can make you feel inferior without
your consent."

We women must get ourselves more self-esteem—and less self that's steam, meaning a self that can go from feeling hot to feeling like nothing within a five-minute phone call.

Buddha backs me up on this:

"In people with no confidence the Dharma
[one's life mission] will produce no result just as
a burnt seed will never produce a green shoot."

This confidence is essential when it comes to dealing with what I consider to be the most hateful word in the English language. A truly ugly, ugly word. The word:

Almost

As in . . .

I almost sold a novel.

Or even worse . . .

I almost won the Nobel peace prize.

Or even worse . . .

I almost met and slept with Andy Garcia.

Almost. I hate that word. The only way to deal with this bitter pill *almost* is with a megadose of confidence. It will give you the extra energy and spirit required to keep going and going and going, like the Energizer Bunny—or John Travolta. Robert Louis Stevenson wrote about this. He said:

> *"To know what you prefer, instead of humbly*
> *saying Amen to what the world tells you you*
> *ought to prefer, is to have kept your soul alive."*

Men know how to do this better than women. Men know one strike doesn't mean you're out—or one bad game doesn't mean you're bad. Sometimes men don't even notice that they've played a bad ball game. They think their performance was peak.

And that goes for other ball games, too.

Yes, I was just being catty. Sorry. Couldn't resist.

My point is: It never ceases to amaze me the bottomless reservoir of self-confidence that the men in my life have displayed, whereas I've witnessed all too many terrific women get down on themselves way too quickly after small setbacks. These are women who don't have:

> *unconditional self-love*

but rather . . .

> *conditional self-love.*

Or even worse:

> *unrequited self-love.*

Women learned this love lesson from their very first self-love affair —the one they had with society when they were little girls. For many, this was quite the dysfunctional love affair.

However, before you start feeding your ego How-to-Handle-a-Hungry-Man-Size portions of sustenance, consider . . .

THERE ARE DISADVANTAGES TO THIS MALE ADVANTAGE

I once joked with my boyfriend Josh that his two favorite words to hear were "You're right." He laughed and admitted that these words were indeed a real turn-on for him. They are for other men as well. In fact, a good business venture might be a 1-900-U-R-RIGHT phone line: Call up anytime, day or night, and hear just how right you are, oh, yeah, baby!

This love of being right is both positive (a confidence sign) and negative (a stop sign—MEANING . . . a Mr. I'm Right Complex can stop new ideas and insights from penetrating—as well as reality from penetrating). MEANING . . . whereas many women have trouble saying that tongue tangler "no," many men have trouble *hearing* "no." For many a man . . .

No = yes.

Except when he is the one saying "no," then . . .

No = fuck off.

When you let your ego rule, you can find yourself having trouble differentiating between:

what *is right*

and

who *is right*

It's funny. Our modern-day lingo has an expression about egotistical people:

He thinks he's all that.

108

Ancient seers also had an expression:

*"I am that, you are that, all this is that, and
that's all there is."*

In other words, get over yourself. You're just a mass of carbon and hydrogen like everyone else.

I know I told you it's not good to live in the past, BUT remember back to that time we shared in my Introduction? Remember the part where I mentioned how the ego can ruin our chance for clarity—and a potential good joke?

Well, it's true. At times I think the ego should be called the not-so-super-ego. In the corporate boardroom of the mind, we should not be voting the ego in as such a big guy in charge. Instead, he should be second in charge and our CEOs should be our spirit and our heart—or what the Buddhists call the Higher Self. Those of us stuck with the ego as CEO wind up with a bratty tyrant who makes a lot of stupid decisions and foolishly gives our Higher Self mostly menial tasks when it could be doing some phenomenal work that would lead to growth and profit for our internal infrastructure.

In Carlos Castaneda's book *The Art of Dreaming*, Don Juan explains the benefits that people experience when they demote the ego from the CEO position:

*"Most of our energy goes into upholding our
importance. . . . If we were capable of losing
some of that importance, two extraordinary
things would happen to us. One, we would free
our energy from trying to maintain the illusory
idea of our grandeur; and two, we would provide
ourselves with enough energy . . . to catch a
glimpse of the actual grandeur of the universe."*

If you are feeling empty inside even though by society's standards you're successful, it is most likely because your *ego* is *too successful*. Demote her. Give your higher self a huge promotion. Productivity will soar—both at work and at play. And your accountant will approve of this promotion/demotion deal, since you'll soon have more savings, because your ego is a poor money manager. He's the one who's been running amok with your credit cards, charging up those Prada bags (or, in my case, Barry Kisselstein Cord bags—the pocketbook equivalent of Andy Garcia).

Staremaster
For Stronger, Healthier Egos

1. Make a deal with yourself: No footprints on the face—yours or anyone else's.

2. Get to know a man's E-spot—his ego-spot, that is. Wherever he displays too much bravura, he is really a scared puppy. Overconfidence is usually underconfidence, and a good business opportunity for a business gal to kick butt in. And as Sun Tzu says:

   "Be deferential to foster their arrogance . . .
   attack where they are unprepared."

3. As I mentioned in Part 1, a good ego-building exercise is visualization. Imagine yourself being congratulated for a job well done—or being promoted to a higher level. Tell yourself: Somebody's got to get this acknowledgment and/or promotion, so that somebody might as well be me.

4. Practice that tongue twister:

   No

Use it as a mantra: no, no, no, no, no. And know that all these "no's" will eventually get you more "YES!" in your life.

5. If you're truly having a problem with self-confidence, consider therapy. Get in touch with your childhood programming—then switch to a better network.

6. Remember what Anais Nin said:

   "Life shrinks or expands according to one's courage."

   And what Woolite said:

   "pH balanced so as to prevent shrinkage."

   And a balanced ego means you don't need a shrink.

7

THE BEST THINGS IN
LIFE ARE FEES

*U*nlike women, men have no trouble talking about money. It's right up there with "sex" and "you're right" as big conversational turn-ons. In fact, yet another great business venture might be a 1-900-MONEY phone line: Hear all about huge, throbbing wads of money, stiff stacks of bills, softly, rounded numbers, twenty-four hours a day!

We women, however, have trouble with money talk. This monetary prudery came to us about the same time as:

Grades: a kid's Monopoly version of money

For students, grades hold value and status. Straight A's are the teenager's equivalent of a six-figure income. Boys flash theirs. Girls flush over theirs. I personally was teased about my high math grades—meaning I was being taught, along with trigonometry, that if I wanted to be liked, I shouldn't succeed too greatly. That one plus the other did not add up, but divided me from my peers.

Same goes for big girls and big salaries.

We are conditioned to feel guilty about both shining at the office and asking for more money *because* we're shining at the office—as if this would makes us greedy or crude. This condition only gets further reinforced due to conversational atrophy. For instance . . .

A True Urban Love Story

I once dated this guy—cute—very cute even—
but he was like a human piñata. It was hard
getting him to open up and reveal personal
information—basic stuff about his mother, his
father, if he ever had a dog as a kid. I jokingly
asked him if he was with the Witness Relocation
Program. (He claimed not.) Me, I was fine with
telling him ALL about my mom and dad, and
how I'd always wanted a dog but had to settle
for cats who I then raised to be like dogs. So,
after dinner, we go up to my apartment for
coffee. (I swear. That's all. Okay, maybe also a
biscotti. But that's it.)
    "So," he said, "do you own your apartment?"
    Now it was my turn to get conversationally
claustrophobic.
    "Uh, yeah," I said.
    "How much did you pay for it?" he asked.
    I didn't want to answer.
    He pushed.
    Ironically, the same way I had continued to
push him to tell me about his family and love
life, he pushed me to tell him about my monthly
mortgage payments. And the same way he had
had trouble answering, I had trouble answering.
Meanwhile, he was more than forthcoming
about telling me what he had paid for his apart-

ment—and the retail value of anything in it.

"Let me get this right," I said to him. "You won't tell me about your relationship with your mother, but you'd feel comfortable showing me your tax returns from last year."

"Yeah," he said. "So?"

That's when I realized men and women are different. Well, that's not when I FIRST realized it. (That's another story, one that involves my brother, a bathtub, and what I thought at first was a sunken toy battleship.) ANYWAY . . . my point is:

Girls practice talking about personal relationship stuff with one another, so we feel comfortable talking about this.

Guys practice talking about money stuff with one another, so they feel comfortable talking about that.

Girls with that money stuff can scare off guys in personal relationships (as I mentioned in Part 1), whereas guys attract more personal relationship stuff the more they have money. Yet another reason girls don't feel comfortable talking money and guys do.

It also hurts a girl's confidence about money when she sees other women around her consistently being given a lower career market value than men—priced at seventy-one cents to a man's dollar. Similarly, it emboldens a man's money confidence to see other men around him earning a shitload of money—which, by the way, is my favorite number: "a shitload." What a swell number to earn.

ANYWAY . . . A woman's "seventy-one cents to a man's dollar" market value subliminally reinforces her insecurity about her earning worth, which can lead to a downward money/self-esteem spiral. For the same self-image reasons I mentioned earlier about why the rich get richer, those who are paid less money eventually see themselves as worth less money, thereby leading to them asking for less money, etc., etc.

Thankfully, an upward money/self-esteem spiral also exists, as I realized early on in my advertising career. It was amusing to me how the more I didn't want to write ads, the more money I'd ask for in hopes of scaring away employers—and instead, the more jobs and money I'd attract.

But before you go stampeding into your boss's office with your pay stub and an abacus, keep in mind . . .

THERE ARE DISADVANTAGES TO THIS MALE ADVANTAGE

Single-minded greed is a biggie disadvantage. As the Buddhist expression goes:

"Desire blinds us like the pickpocket who sees only the saint's pockets."

As I mentioned in Part 1, when you're holding the latest Bendel's catalog in your hands, you can forget to remember the real things of value in life. Ultimately it's not your external riches that satisfy but rather the rewards of investing in a rich internal world, and . . .

Finding out how the other half of YOU lives.

There's an old joke:

If you want to know what God thinks of money, just look at some of the people he gives it to.

Actually, it's no joke. It won't matter if you manage to double your salary if your spirit and true self are sacrificed in the process. All you will do is:

Upgrade your restaurants, not upgrade your life.

You will wind up merely feeling a sense of despair and longing while dining on lobster instead of feeling a sense of despair and longing while dining on tuna noodle casserole. If you let it, your ego will convince you that this menu change is a life improvement, but you will merely be attaining an outer symbol of success, without attaining your inner career goal: your Career Waldo.

I know. Every year I kept postponing quitting the ad business to pursue my writing dreams because I had gotten another raise. And every year my dining and whining improved at a simultaneous rate. My art director and I used to talk about how we lived in a golden cage. A running joke was:

If you can't come in on Saturday, don't bother coming in on Sunday.

The irony was we were earning big money but had little free time during which to spend it. But I suppose that's the reason why God created Victoria's Secret catalogs. Then again, God also created "the weekend" and "sloth," two marvelous concepts which I was not getting the opportunity to explore.

This was no way to live. I know that now. I've been rich and I've been poor, and believe me, *both* can suck.

My art director at the time was on Prozac, which made him lose both his hair and sexual desire. At first he worried about these side effects—especially the latter. But then he realized that not being horny all the time freed him up to get more work done, and thereby continue to make more money.

One day he realized he didn't need more funds—but more fun. He started taking time off, and soon he didn't need the Prozac. Fun was more gratifying than funds, especially funds he was too busy to find time to spend anyway.

There are many folks in the ad business—as well as plenty of other businesses—who are so busy working hard to make lots o' cash in order

116

to live a better life that, ironically, they don't have time to spend it in order to get this "better life."

My Big Point—which was also a Part 1 Point—and should be a Big Part of Your One Life Point:

Never stay in a job or pick a job just for the money alone.

As business guru and author Richard Rybolt says:

"Find a job you truly love, and you will never work another day in your life."

Staremaster
For Building Monetary Muscles

1. Always let the other party put in their monetary offer first— then Wonderbra the offer up. Meaning: Add padding, padding, padding.
2. It's okay to accept a job at the company of your dreams for less money—or even an internship for no money, if you can afford it. ALWAYS think: long-term greed over short-term greed. The most important thing is to get your foot in the *right* door. Once you're in, you can wander around and gather clues on how to strengthen your position. As Sun Tzu says:

"The wise general seeks his grain within the territory of the enemy."

3. Whenever money is at stake, ALWAYS get it in writing. A mere promise is never as solid of a commitment as a tangible, three-dimensional promissory note.
4. When you ask for a raise, never ask based on your personal needs (meaning: I have a baby) or your competitor's pay

(meaning: I *am* a baby) but only on your merits, your own self-worth.

5. Relax if you're not making hand-over-fist gobs of cash. As business book author Rybolt says, "The best job security is to be worth more than you are paid."

6. If you can't get them to give you the money you want, don't cut off negotiations. Try instead to barter with other things, like free product or extra vacation time.

7. Check out what the other guy's expenses are—where is his money most spent—and you'll learn about his vulnerabilities. For instance: Does he spend his money on vacations with his wife or margaritas with teenage models at the downtown clubs?

8. Lesser fees will usually amount to lesser respect, not more work opportunities. Just like with designer goods, the higher the price, the higher the view of worth.

9. Don't round off numbers when you put in a bid. It makes it seem as if you haven't spent time adding up real costs.

10. Think about investing some of your money for a rainy day—or a sunny weekend in Florida. Read and be inspired by the Beardstown Ladies, who offer wise investment advice. Or call my two favorite stockbrokers, my dad (Rubin) or my brother (Eric) at Smith Barney, at 1-800-233-1414, ext. 6280.

11. Look into switching your high-interest-rate credit cards to low-interest-rate credit cards—and keep switching. Credit card companies are always eager to lure you away from other credit card companies with competitive rates. Go for it.

12. Whenever you're asked your fee or salary rate, ask the other person to tell you the number they're thinking first. You never know. They could offer you more than you were going to suggest.

13. If possible, keep detailed files of your spending from week to week so at tax time you won't be overwhelmed with organizing your expenses.

14. It's worth it to invest some of your money in corporate gifts not only at Christmastime but also after big projects are completed —but don't give gifts that are so lavish they seem like corporate bribery or marriage proposals.

15. In case you haven't noticed, the economy sucks—but this is good for the ladies, because it means guys are more open to us bringing in that second paycheck.

8

ACKNOWLEDGE
IS POWER

*M*ost men know how to accept compliments. Often these compliments are even ones a man heaps upon himself. No matter. He's a heaper. Women, however, are light heapers.

For example, here's a . . .

SURPRISE QUIZ

You've just received the following compliment:

"Wow, you look really *good today."*

You say:

a. Thank you.
b. Thank you . . . for giving me a compliment I don't deserve.
c. Really? That must be because you remember me uglier.

If you answered b or c, you are a typical woman, meaning you have a tendency to rebroadcast your childhood programming—programming that includes popular hits from the past such as:

FATHER AND SON KNOW BEST
I DREAM OF BEING A PERFECT LITTLE GIRL
THE LADY BUNCH
SHHH. KEEP IT DOWN.

Guys are better at acknowledging compliments because they grew up bragging, flexing, showing off. Even boy toys more than girlie toys call out more for attention: blabbering BB guns, loud bouncing basketballs, plastic/paper airplanes that could poke your eye out. Even a boy's insult is acknowledged as a compliment. After a really good basketball maneuver you might hear:

Boy 1: You suck, you scumbucket.
Boy 2: Thanks, man.

Then they'd slap five.
Plus . . .

Think About It

Culturally speaking, girls don't even have their own femalesque hand signal, like "a slap you five." Girls never needed one, because girls blush—avoiding acknowledgment—whereas boys slap five—acknowledging acknowledgment.

Boys grew up knowing there's no benefit in *not* acknowledging one's positive attributes. In case this is still not entirely clear to you, imagine . . .

President Clinton has just been told by Gloria Steinem that he did a great job making sure more women get equal pay. (Okay, well, I guess we should start with imagining Clinton doing such a thing. But let's say he has.) Imagine this scene:

A Scene in the Oval Office

> Gloria Steinem: *Thanks, President Clinton. You really did a marvelous thing. You're doing a great job as president.*
> Clinton: *Oh, no. Not really. I mean, I'm an okay president. Maybe. Uh . . . You think I'm doing okay? Jeez. Really?*

As you can see, modesty is not a very male attribute—or helpful attribute in the workplace.

Another tendency women have more than men is to point out a weakness of their own before the other person even notices it. For instance:

> A Woman: *I gained weight, I know. Look —* look—*do you see this? Look at my tummy—my middle, my whole middle, it's totally fat—specifically in this area. See?*

Again, imagine President Clinton:

> Clinton: *I might have done well with that new work bill, but look—*look—*do you see this part of my tax plan? Look at the middle class—look at the middle. See how the middle is in trouble —specifically in this area? See?*

Clinton wouldn't do it because he wisely knows there's a chance no one would ever see his weak areas, so why bring attention to them in the first place? Plus, Clinton knows that if you offer up doubt, the other person may begin to doubt his or her initial judgment of you, and/or be offended that *you* doubt his or her judgment.

Another problem females face more than males is juggling all our identities. A woman's under pressure to do/be everything: a respected professional, beauty queen, sex goddess, surrogate therapist to friends, aerobics star, and cookie-baking mom. It's easy for a woman to find a motive for not acknowledging her successes along the way: by thinking about everything else she still has to do and be.

I personally have this goofy propensity: Even when things are going really, really well, I can always find something I could have done better. Or, if I accept that perhaps I did achieve a fantasy goal, I immediately worry that I've set a new standard for myself that I won't be able to meet again. All too often this perfectionism is not really about—nor does it even lead toward—

bettering ourselves

but rather to . . .

embittering ourselves.

It comes from the urge to look for the worst, while ignoring the best, which comes from that irksome little devil: self-sabotaging insecurity. We women need to get ourselves . . .

An Acknowledge Education

We can learn a lot from watching men and witnessing how unabashed they are about telling you their accomplishments—or sending self-promoting memos around the office or to newspapers. As Gracián says:

"When you have both talent and a talent for displaying your gifts, the result is something prodigious."

Don't be shy. If you let others know what you are capable of, they might serendipitously know about another rewarding job opportunity for you.

But before you start painting the Goodyear blimp with your photo image, consider . . .

THERE ARE DISADVANTAGES TO THIS MALE ADVANTAGE

*Y*ou can suffer from a bad credit rating.

Some people overborrow credit—they take the credit outright from someone else who better deserves it. Or they say "I" when perhaps they should be saying "we." They suffer from what I call:

An "I" Disease

This "I" disease affects the cornea of their insights. They're blind to how others have contributed to their success. Luckily, there is . . .

A Cure for "I Disease":

a clunk in the head

It works. Try it out on someone with this infliction. You'll see. And hopefully he'll start to see better, too.

Another problem with acknowledgment: a person can over-acknowledge the work he's done—raise another's expectations of what has been accomplished, which can eventually lower credibility—or make people question his taste or intelligence level.

Or a fella looking for a little acknowledgment can suffer from:

Pre-jocular-ation

He preacknowledges his good work—before the work is even done —or *good.* So . . .

Make sure the hype is ripe.

Make sure the time to give the hype is ripe, too. As Gracián say:

"Ostentation doesn't work when it is done out of season."

If someone else is busy sunning himself in the spotlight, don't try to upstage him.

$\mathcal{S}$*taremaster*
For Acknowledgment

1. After you've done a good job, acknowledge it silently to yourself. If it's true we women are naturally nurturing, we must learn to turn that nurturing inward: let ourselves enjoy our successes. A good first step toward this goal is to incorporate the following mantra into your corporate life. After finishing/while having trouble finishing a report or a presentation, repeat silently to yourself:

   "Damn, I'm good. Damn, I'm good. Damn,
   I'm good. Damn, I'm good. Damn, I'm good."

   Or do as the comic actor/writer/director Eric Schaeffer did in one of his movies: Give yourself a "self high five." The way to do it is . . .

   1. First, make sure you are alone—unlike Schaeffer.
   2. Like Schaeffer, raise one hand high to the other, and slap them together with self-contented glee.

2. Whenever you've accomplished something you feel proud about, put a star on that date in your calendar.*
3. Play Good Cop/Good Cop. Whenever possible, try to set up that ideal situation where you have a coworker do your bragging for you and you do the bragging for your coworker.

---

*NOTE: Make sure this star is different from the star you use to mark your menstrual cycle or you could get very confused—and/or pregnant.

4. Remember: NEVER be the first to point out your weaknesses to your boss or coworkers. If they tend to notice the bad stuff, then they'll notice the bad stuff. If they don't, shhhhhhhhhh.

5. Remember that commotion = promotion or else you should consider some locomotion.

6. In your journal, write two lists of your best qualities. The first list should include your obvious BEST. The second should be made up of those qualities you take for granted. I believe you can sometimes wind up ignoring your best qualities because they come so easy.

   For instance:

   a. Whenever I share an appetizer with a friend, I am fair about only eating my equitable half.

   or

   b. I have nice feet. Some people have really ugly feet. Not me.

   or

   c. I know what the word *prolix* means.

7. Put Your Face in Their Face—send out self-promoting memos to the newspaper or trade journals. Don't wait for your company to do it.

8. In advertising, there's something called "Reach and Frequency." This means FIRST make sure your message goes out to the RIGHT TARGET AUDIENCE. In the corporate sphere, this usually means the higher-ups. SECOND, keep making sure. Reach them with that high-frequency wave of good PR.

9. The best way to gain acknowledgment is to make others think they have decided on their own to give it to you. So be SUBTLE in exposing all your good work.

10. Women know how to accessorize outfits with cosmetics and

pretty baubles. Men know how to accessorize stories with hyperbole and pretty babble. Be particularly wary of the credit people claim that they have performed. No matter how convincingly a guy tells you about "how big the fish is that he caught," always ask to see the fish.

9

BELIEVING IN A
LAUGHTER LIFE

*I*t's a funny thing, this funny thing. Men are better known for being adept at it than women—especially business-oriented feminists. Whatever "feminist" means.*

There's even a lightbulb joke that exemplifies this prejudicial attitude, and I believe lightbulb jokes are *theee* most revealing barometer of this country's prejudices—more revealing than any report in *Time* magazine or on CNN.

Important American
Attitudinal Barometer

Question: *How many feminists does it take to put in a lightbulb?*
Answer: *One—and that's NOT funny, dammit.*

*NOTE: Why did the word *feminist* lose all of its positive connotations so quickly? I believe it's a sign of this country's nonacceptance of feminism as a concept.

You'd never hear that joke about men who are "male feminists," whatever that means. I guess it would mean smart, equality-minded guys.*

Let's rewrite the above joke to apply to this kind of man:

> Question: *How many "smart, equality-minded*
> *guys" does it take to put in a lightbulb?*
> Answer: *One—and that's NOT funny, dammit.*

And indeed it is NOT funny. Basically, society just doesn't expect "smart, equality-minded wo<u>men</u>" to be joking.

A Ha-Ha-Ha-Hawaii Story

> *I was in Hawaii with a guy I was dating. A*
> *storekeeper asked us if we were married.*
> *"Well . . . Not to each other," I said.*
> *I made a few more quips. Then the store-*
> *keeper said to my paramour (I love that word):*
> *"You're a funny guy."*
> *Meanwhile, my paramour had not said one*
> *joke. The storekeeper had noticed humor ema-*
> *nating from us somewhere—he just didn't*
> *remember exactly from where, and assumed it*
> *was from the male in the duo.*

Men of all kinds, all demographic groups, are known for loving a good laugh—and a good laugh is known for loving these laughing men right back. According to Dr. Lee S. Berk of the Loma Linda School of Public Health in California:

> *"An hour spent laughing lowers the levels of*
> *stress hormones like cortisol and epinephrine.*
> *At the same time, the immune system appears*

---

*NOTE: Why isn't there a popular word for this kind of man?

129

to grow stronger, the body's T-cells, natural
killer cells and antibodies all show signs of
heightened activity."

There are many benefits to hooting it up at the office. Indeed, if it is truly true that men enjoy a good laugh more than women, we should join in on all the laughter. After all . . .

Laughter Is Good Medicine . . . and Then Some
1. Laughter Is a Health Enhancer
2. Laughter Is a Creativity Builder
3. Laughter Is a Social Glue
4. Laughter Is a Good Personal-Invasion Evasion
5. Laughter Is a Good Enlightening Agent for Criticism or Prejudices
6. Laughter Is a Good Calorie Burner

With all these benefits, a woman should be eager to join in on all the fun and festivities that laughter brings.

Admittedly, however, many women are afraid of making jokes. I suppose it's because joking means risking, putting yourself out there, and perhaps not getting the laugh track of approval you want. PLUS . . . it's doubly hard to have a good laugh-track record if you're a woman.

Basically, joking goes against a female's socialization: Nice girls blend in. They don't draw attention to themselves—and being a jokester does the opposite.

But when a joke is good, it's very, very good. To quote a March 1996 article in *The New York Times* on the benefits of laughter:

"Few behaviors, short of shouting 'Fire!' in a
movie theater, can have such a dramatic
swelling impact on group behavior as can a
burst of merry chime of laughter."

But before you get out your whoopee cushions, remember . . .

THERE ARE DISADVANTAGES
TO THIS MALE ADVANTAGE

*I*f you're always joking, eventually people will have trouble taking you seriously. This rule also holds true for products and commercials. Years back, Alka-Seltzer ran some highly hysterical commercials—the ones with those memorable moments like with the guy named Ralph who could not believe he might have eaten the whole thing, and that other one with an actor playing an actor who kept having to eat all those "speecy meta-a-ball-as." Remember? I do. These spots were so funny, they were the reason I wanted to enter the field of advertising. Later, when in the field, I learned that during the time these popular and loved spots ran, Alka-Seltzer sales *decreased.* The reason? Consumers thought the spots were so funny, they had trouble taking Alka-Seltzer seriously. They felt the product must not be such a serious and therefore hard-working product. You, too, could suffer from the same fate if you're too jokey at the office.

Another potential danger of humor is intimidation. This humor rule increases manifold when the humor in question is about a guy—and comes from a girl. I know. My last book was practically a research project that tested whether a man can take a joke directed at him from a woman. As I mentioned, this book was called:

> *How to Make Your Man Behave in 21 Days or*
> *Less, Using the Secrets of Professional Dog*
> *Trainers*

Though it could just as easily have been called:

> *How to Make Some Men Really Fidgety in Your*
> *Presence*

After this book was published, I found out something very quickly:

> *Men have feelings, too.*

Well, maybe that's an exaggeration. It's more like:

Men have "feeling"—in the singular.

Just kidding, just kidding. Jeez, I must have said "Just kidding, just kidding" a gazillion times since my "doggie book" came out. But it *does* seem that all too often a man's least favorite kind of joke is one made at his expense BY A WOMAN—because this expense puts a dent in his respect and power budget.

Dr. Provine, a professor of neurobiology, psychology, and the anthropology of laughter at the University of Maryland, Baltimore County, would most likely agree with me. As he has said already:

> *"Fashions on laughter change, but one thing*
> *that stays the same is you can't laugh at people*
> *in power. Laugh at your boss, and you may be*
> *the recipient of that practical joke known as*
> *the little pink slip."*

A March 1996 article in *The New York Times* pointed out how powerful humor can be—so much so, that during the Nazi era in Germany the Gestapo kept an extra watchful eye on German comedians fearing the impact of their punchlines.

So if you plan to use humor, remember to use it wisely. Humor might be good medicine, but REMEMBER . . . there are warnings on most medicine bottle labels.

Staremaster
For Building Up That Gut So
You Can Bust It with Laughter

1. Rent a laugh. After a hard day at the office, if nothing at all seems funny, rent a funny film and artificially induce some laughter.

2. If you joke at the office about someone or something, be sure that you let them know you're ONLY JOKING. And be careful that there is not too much truth in the jest, or an "Only kidding" might not be a good enough antidote. Milan Kundera wrote a book called *The Joke,* about a guy who made the wrong joke to the Communist Party—life was no party thereafter.

3. Check out humor as an "Invasion/Evasion Technique." It can get you out of difficult questions. When people ask me, "Do you mind if I ask you how old you are?" I answer, "No, not all. You can ask. It's just the answering part that I mind." I've found this to be the perfect answer to that "age old" question.

4. Humor also makes a good "Enlightening Agent." To quote Laurence J. Peter (a reference listed in *Peter's Quotations*—I'm not sure if he's *theee* Peter)

"An individual is as strong as his or her prejudice. Two things reduce prejudice—education and laughter."

5. Watch out for too much self-deprecating humor at the office. It can eventually diminish your power. I myself have to watch it sometimes. I'm the first person to make a self-deprecating joke. And the second person. And the third person.

6. The next time something pisses you off at the office, always keep in mind that the difference between tragedy and comedy is about three months and five margaritas.

7. If that STILL doesn't work, consult a humor doctor. Really. Dr. Jean Morreal, philosopher, laugh consultant, and president of a firm called Humorworks, believes there are financial gains to be had by laughing on the job. He is helping corporations to believe likewise. His clients include Kodak, Xerox, and the IRS (thank you, thank you for that last one, Dr. Morreal!).

10

BOYS DON'T HAVE
CURFEWS

A businesswoman who stays at the office too late will be majorly
tsk-tsked. Meanwhile, guys don't have a curfew on coming home from
the office. Or if they do, it's a MUCH later curfew than a woman gets—
and men get it without all the guilt.

The Ten-Minute Man

I had a second date with this guy—we'll call
him J. (and we'll never call him again). So J.
has to work late—as do I. We agree he'll pick
me up at my apartment at 8:45 P.M.

He arrives. On time. But I'm running late
due to work. I'd been expecting an important
call from those #$@!& L.A. producers at 6:30
P.M. They call at 8:20 P.M.—with complicated
contract run-around stuff. When J. buzzes (or
rather calls me from his car phone from his car
downstairs) I'm still on the phone with those
#$@! L.A. producers.

*I say, "Oh no! Is it eight forty-five already!?
I'm still doing work—with those #$@! L.A.
producers I told you about. They're giving me
the run-around AGAIN! I'll be down as fast I
can—I'm sorry!"*

*I refresh my makeup and run downstairs,
which equals a total of ten minutes that I kept
J. waiting in his car.*

*J. greets me with "Are you passive
aggressive?"*

*I think he's joking. I say, "No, I'm aggressive
aggressive. There's nothing passive about me."*

*He then says, "I can't believe you kept me
waiting. You didn't even bother getting ready
for me, getting dressed up for our date."*

*"I'm sorry. I'm sorry I'm late. I had a
chaotic workday. These $%#@ producers are at
it again."*

*"You should have been ready for me when I
arrived," J. said.*

*"Look, J., I wish I didn't have to be working.
Believe me, I wish I hadn't been. I'm sorry."*

*But J. remained angry—the whole night. He
wouldn't get past it.*

*"It was narcissistic of you to keep me wait-
ing downstairs," he said. "As if your time was
more important than mine."*

*What I found interesting was that J. thought
I was the one being narcissistic when he was
the one thinking that my working late was on
purpose and revolved around him. In reality,
this meant he was being narcissistic—and*

*insensitive as well by giving me an unrelenting
hard time when I was already in a lousy mood
because of those L.A. producers.*

This work curfew business starts in childhood. As I mentioned in Part 1, a teenaged boy is allowed to play, play, play outside his house until late at night. The typical teenaged girl, however, has a curfew on her playtime, and that potential stigma hovering over her head should she stay out too late.

In womanhood things don't change much. For many men, work is still considered a man's main territory. After all, a man has NO CHOICE. He is expected to work.

On the other hand, society doesn't necessarily expect women to work because they are also expected to have children.

Because a woman is seen as having a choice—to work or not to work—a woman working could be considered a slight extravagance — by some guys (e.g., J.).

However, before you start wishing you could work 24/7 without all the guilt, consider . . .

THERE ARE DISADVANTAGES TO THIS MALE ADVANTAGE

*Y*ou could wind up with Late Night *Without* David Letterman—and no time to cash in on all those blessed frequent-flyer miles. Some folks confuse "working hard" with "working too hard." Usually this happens when they're trying to avoid facing up to their feelings—or a scary issue in their life. Workaholics are not much different from other "–aholics." They pour themselves a few hours of work, like some people pour themselves Stolis.

I know. I am a recovered workaholic. Ironically, I was trying to avoid facing up to how much I hated my job—so I put even more time into my job. Clever of me, huh?

I can't totally blame me. The hours in advertising were sadistic. I remember once my art director and I left the office at 8 P.M., and I said to him, "Oh, good, we got out early tonight." And I meant it. I started to believe that 8 P.M. was an early, easy day.

That's part of the reason I was SO annoyed with those %$#! L.A. producers, because I don't want to return to my old workaholic days— or rather nights. I firmly believe:

> *You need to have a life in your life.*
> *That's why they call it "life."*

Workaholics go through life as if they are "doing life": working long, hard hours trapped in that "golden cage" prison otherwise known as "a corner office"—though it should *really* be known as a "cornered in" office.

It bugs me out when I think about all the wasted time I put into overworking at the office. Then I think about how I'm wasting time thinking about all that wasted time, so I stop.

I now know—and remind myself to keep on knowing—it's called:

AN OCCUPATION,

not

A PREOCCUPATION.

It's called:

SUCCESS,

not

OBSESS.

It's called:

BEING IN A BUSINESS,

137

not

As Robert Frost said:

We dance around in a ring and suppose
but the Secret sits in the middle
and knows.

There's a problem with all that dancing around in a ring. It can make you so dizzy you lose your clarity. MEANING . . . often you can get more work done by getting less work done. As Theodore Roethke said:

"A mind too active is no mind at all."

Too much work can lead to a haziness of mind, which can lead to mistakes, which can lead to you having to do the work all over again— which reminds me of a wonderful parable from Stephen Covey's *The Seven Habits of Highly Effective People*:

I Came, I Sawed, I Concurred

A man is sawing away at a tree, when his
buddy drops by and asks what he's up to. The
guy tells him he can't really talk to him, 'cause
he's busy sawing away at the tree. His buddy
points out that his saw's edge looks a little
dull, and that he could probably saw faster if
he took the time to sharpen it. The guy explains
that he can't stop to sharpen the saw because
he has to saw down the tree.

If you are feeling overwhelmed with work at the office, consult your Career Waldo. Refer back and forth between it and your "to do" list. All of the things on your "to do" list that don't truly lead to your attaining your Career Waldo can be shifted over to your "to do later" list. As the Tao says:

> *"Through taking no unnecessary action, any-thing can be accomplished."*

If you are having trouble sorting out your priorities, it could be helpful to take a meditation break. It will help you to relax and thereby see more clearly. And remember, exhaustion, though on many levels is similar in feel to relaxation, *does not* count as relaxation.

Staremaster
For the Overworked and Overwhelmed

1. If you're a workaholic, read the twelve-step program from Alcoholics Anonymous and wherever it says "alcohol," replace it with the word *work*.
2. Try to respond to all office mail and phone calls as they come in—and only once. As the Taoists say: "Governing . . . is like frying a small fish . . . you can't turn it over too often. If turned over too many times, the fish will fall apart." So don't flip around your verbal communication so many times you lose your original power, or those sentences in your reports so much they lose their original flavor.
3. If you're given a dorky, menial, insulting task, speak up. Don't be a martyr. Be smartyr.
4. Give yourself vacations as a reward for hard work. And don't bring work with you on the vacation—or turn the vacation into work. I went to a spa with a workaholic girlfriend, who overscheduled her massages, facials, exercise classes. Ironi-

cally, she was just as busy and stressed out trying to make all her spa appointments as she had been in the office trying to make all her work appointments!

5. Schedule "fun appointments" with the same commitment to them as you have for work appointments.

Part 3

SUPPORT FOR

BOOBS IN

BUSINESS

———

IN THE
DRESSING ROOM OF
THE HEART, THE WILL
HAS A SEPARATE
CHANGING AREA

*T*his section should be one of your favorites in this book, because you don't have to learn anything. Nothing. *Nada.* No learning at all required.

Just un-learning.

What follows are un-lessons, in which I'll be doing some un-teaching of the fraudulent lessons society has wrongly taught women—in particular, the lesson that we should be ashamed of our female qualities, not only in general in life, but especially in our *career life*. We must un-learn viewing our female qualities as inequalities at the office. We women have many unique female attributes and talents that are not only wonderful, but in many cases *superior advantages over men* in the career marketplace.

The good news is: We don't have to learn how to use these attributes and talents. We already innately know how. We just have to un-learn the values and prejudicial judgments society has granted them. Which reminds me of:

A Light and Death Situation

I have this fluorescent light fixture in my bath-
room that keeps burning out bulbs every few
months. It happened again just this week. I was
going to buy another bulb, but hadn't found
time. My friend Sherwin was over. When he
exited my bathroom, this supposedly dead bulb
was shining brightly.
"It just needed a little jiggle," he explained.

The same goes for YOU. You don't necessarily need to run out and buy new attributes for yourself. You have all the attributes you need for success right inside you—all that light, just waiting to shine. You just need to give yourself a jiggle.

More good news: This jiggle is not much of a change.

Some bad news: This jiggle still falls under the category of "a change."

Some bad to worse news: Unfortunately, change is a two-step process, beginning with:

1. Knowing one should change.
2. Doing the actual change.

It's that second aspect of change that's the doozy to do. Lieh-Tzu writes about this tricky second step in *A Taoist Guide to Practical Living*:

Some Taoist Cliffs Notes

There was this guy who knew the secret to
immortality. There was another guy, Hu-tzu,
who lived in a distant kingdom, who thought
that was a good thing to know, so he set out on

144

*a journey to meet this immortality expert. When
Hu-tzu arrived, a local dude told him that the
immortality expert had just DIED. Hu-tzu was
very disappointed. The local dude teased
Hu-tzu, saying, "Why be disappointed?
Obviously this so-called immortality expert
was a fake. I mean, if he knew the secret to
immortality, why is he dead?" Hu-tzu dis-
agreed, saying, "There are some people who
know the principles of a skill yet cannot apply
it. There are some people who can apply the
principles without knowing what they are.
Knowledge must come before action, but action
does not necessarily come before knowledge. It
is a rare case that someone both knows the theory and is able to apply it."*

Obviously, the ideal is to have both the knowledge AND the skill to
apply it. I want YOU to have both. There's one skill that, if you develop
it, will better ensure your chances:

The skill of will.

You have to want your Career Waldo badly enough to pay the price
of expended time and energy, potential humiliation, stress, self-doubt,
paramour-doubt, monetary distress—WHATEVER. You must have the
will to keep going until knowledge of change and actual change merge.

A Coronary Corollary

*Put a Post-It note on your heart, reminding you
why you want what you want so badly. Every
time you're lost, look at your heart and remember where you're going and why. AND . . . for*

*those of you who have been spending so much
time in the corporate jungle that you're having
trouble finding your heart, reread your Pep
Talk page. Then reread it again.*

As Buddhist sage Brihadaranyaka Upanishad says:

*You are what your deep, driving desire is.
As your desire is, so is your will.
As your will is, so is your deed.
As your deed is, so is your destiny.*

You will discover, if you haven't already, that this skill of will is the determinator of whether or not you will achieve your career destiny. That gap between "desire" and "will" might seem little, but it's actually quite a biggie—as is that little gap between will and action. Another biggie. The trick to not FALLING IN is to be FILLING IN those gaps with self-love and self-confidence so you can keep moving forward until you reach your destination.

I know a transportation expert who agrees with me, and who gives some further good transportation advice. In the words of The Little Engine That Could:

*"I think I can, I think I can, I think I can, I
know I can, I know I can, I know I can,
choochoo."*

This train should be your constant train of thought as you read the following Top Ten Female Qualities. With this skill of will you can un-learn not to fight against but rather side with your female side in the fight to reach your career destiny.

1

ASKING
INDIRECTIONS

*T*ransvestites are not the only ones feeling awkward playing women here in the nineties. We "au naturel" women are feeling just as inept. The only thing harder than knowing how to be a woman nowadays is knowing how to be a *businesswoman*. We are consistently asking ourselves:

> SHOULD I BE MORE ASSERTIVE WITH MY CLIENT?
> MORE DIRECT WITH MY ASSISTANT?
> MORE DEMANDING WITH MY STAFF?
> IF SO, WILL THEY CONSIDER ME A BITCH?
> AM I BITCH?
> IS IT GOOD TO BE A BITCH?
> SHOULD I ONLY BE MADE OF SUGAR AND SPICE
>   AND EVERYTHING NICE?
> OR SHOULD I THROW IN A FEW SNAILS AND
>   PUPPY DOGS' TAILS?

Sun Tzu gave his recipe for great leadership. It included a mixture of:

Wisdom, trustworthiness, benevolence,
courage, and sternness.

Looks like Sun Tzu was just as confused about the ingredients for success. Two of them seem to contradict each other:

Sternness and *benevolence*

These two qualities represent two polar forces of the management spectrum. On one end there's

sternness,
then all the way on the other end . . .

. . . *benevolence*
can be found.

Most women—with their instinctive desire to be loved and not hurt anybody's feelings—seem to feel most comfy spending their business day on the benevolence end of the spectrum, especially the delegating part of a business day. MEANING. . . .

Women tend to delegate with
fuzzy statements
on that
benevolence
end of the spectrum,

whereas men tend to delegate with
bald commands
on the
sternness
end of the spectrum.

For example, a woman might say:

"Are you going to be on the phone long?
I don't mean to rush you, but . . ."

148

Contrarily, a man might say:

"Get off the phone. I need you to do this ASAP."

Interestingly, I personally might say:

*When I first wrote the above male directive, I
worded it as "Could you get off the phone, please?"
thinking this was an example of a bald command.
Then I realized the "Could you" and a "please"
made it not so bald and not so commandlike. When I
finally wrote "Get off the phone," without those other
word amenities, it sounded mean to me. Yet this is
indeed how a man in power might talk—in a way
that I, as a woman, instinctively don't feel comfortable speaking—or even typing.* *

Other Indirectional Phrases a Woman Might Use

"IT MIGHT BE USEFUL IF . . ."

"MAYBE YOU WOULD WANT TO . . ."

"PERHAPS IT'S ONLY ME, BUT . . ."

"I HAVE A PROBLEM. I REALLY HAVE TO GET THIS
REPORT DONE, BUT . . ."

"IT'S OKAY, I'LL SIT IN THE DARK."

Although some men can be indirect, too, most view "giving indirections" as a sign of female weakness. But these men are missing out
on a powerful negotiating tool. They should not view indirections as . . .

"On-your-knees" management style

---

*I know, HOW ODD, *this* from the same girl who puts the word *penis* in her book title. I'm
a human oxymoron—like "jumbo shrimp" is a crustacean oxymoron.

But rather as . . .

Japanese management style.

According to Deborah Tannen: "The Japanese hold in high regard those who communicate indirectly, implicitly, subtly and even nonverbally, trusting the listener's empathy to fill in meaning." In fact, Tannen goes on to say that the Japanese "believe that only an insensitive, uncouth person needs a direct, verbal, complete message." The Japanese even have three highly respected words devoted to the practice of indirect communication:

> **omoiyara:** EMPATHY. THE JAPANESE BELIEVE THAT
> BECAUSE OF THE BEAUTY OF *omoiyara,* FOLKS
> SHOULD NOT HAVE TO EXPRESS THEIR MEAN-
> ING EXPLICITLY, BECAUSE OTHERS SHOULD
> SENSE THEIR MEANING INTUITIVELY.
>
> **sassuru:** TO ANTICIPATE ANOTHER'S MESSAGE
> INTUITIVELY.
>
> **sasshi:** THE ANTICIPATION OF ANOTHER'S MESSAGE
> THROUGH INSIGHTFUL GUESSWORK. THE
> JAPANESE ALSO BELIEVE THAT *sasshi* IMPLIES
> MATURITY.

All three of these words could simultaneously be apt descriptions for women.

MEANING . . . We women are instinctively displaying Japanese management style, which speaks highly of our speaking indirectly. After all, the Japanese are highly efficient masters at business. So, to all those men who think being baldly direct is where it's at, and being indirect is a sign of female weakness, I say:

Weakness shmeakness, female shmemale.

This indirect form of delegation is working wonders for the Japanese. The proof? Check out all the vast wonders the Japanese are working on. You can read about them in any magazine you find lying around one of our many American unemployment offices.

Rather than viewing indirectness as powerlessness, it can and should be seen as a symbol of powerfulness. Think about Clint Eastwood and all those heroes in kung fu movies. A simple glance or raise of the eyebrow and people clammer to fetch them this, lug them that.

Then there are all those British masters—an example Tannen offered in *Talking from 9 to 5*. A master merely has to comment, "I feel a bit of a draft." The servant dashes to turn on the heat.

Even a toughie like Machiavelli acknowledged that benevolent indirectness has its power, when he said:

> *"Some of the things that appear to be virtues*
> *will, if [a leader] practices them, ruin him, and*
> *some of the things that appear to be vices will*
> *bring him security and prosperity."*

MEANING . . . Being indirect is not necessarily a female vice. It can be a virtue. A woman doesn't have to give commanding orders like a stereotypical American male to get what she wants done.

> *You don't need a penis to take your staff in*
> *hand.*

Admittedly, however, there is an embarrassing side to all this good news about this woman's trait. We women learned indirectness for the wrong reason: fear.

As little girls, we grew up afraid to ask for things directly, so we developed a skill for subtly communicating our desires. We learned that being coy, shy, and diminutive usually got us all the cool stuff we wanted —a vast improvement over what happened whenever we were direct and found ourselves being disliked for our "pushiness" and/or having our requests turned down.

As we grew older, we discovered the situation was not changing much. Society still looked down upon a woman who was direct about her needs and requests. Consider the reactions movie audiences had to . . .

1. The Holly Hunter character in *Broadcast News* who gives the taxi driver specific directions.
2. The Meg Ryan character in *When Harry Met Sally* who tells the waiter specifically how she wants her food.

In both instances, these women were met with disapproval. Luckily for these women, they were living in a comedy movie, so viewers merely found them "endearingly amusing." However, had these women been living in real life, the laughter that greeted them might have had a harder edge.

We women have been taught—and have learned the lesson well— that being indirect has more benefits than directness. Although we women learned this for the *wrong* reasons, we can use this trait to serve a positive and higher purpose:

HELPING OUR CAREERS!

Indirectness can help us do this by . . .

1. **Creating fewer ruffled feathers:** It can protect our office stature in case a request is not granted or even give us the option of totally denying that a request was ever made in the first place—which also means it can protect our relationship with the other person in case they are offended by the request.
2. **Creating more flocking together:** Kinder, gentler wording can infuse a situation with benevolence, a persuasive behavioral motivator. PLUS . . . it can make others feel as if the deed they are motivated

to do was *their* idea, *not ours,* giving them a sense of empowerment, which assistants and clients thrive on.

Madison Avenue also recognizes the persuasive powers of indirectness. In advertising:

> *a* hard *sell*

is usually less effective than:

> *a* soft *sell.*

If you notice, "soft sell" has that word *soft* in there. "Softness" makes for a more powerful sales pitch than hardness.

HOWEVER . . . The most hypnotic kind of advertising sell of all is one so soft you hardly even notice it. This type comes in two forms:

1. **Infomercials:** Is that a TV program or a sales pitch?
2. **Subliminal seduction**: Is that a melting ice cube or a woman's nipple?

Both of the above make two great advertisements for the underlying powers of indirectness. Infomercials sell gazillions of goofy products. Melted ice cubes sell . . . well, they don't sell nipples. Nipples don't need much selling.

BUT . . . I am reminded of a good advertising story about a sexy woman named . . .

Barbie: A Guise and Doll Story

One of my claims to fame is writing a commercial for Barbie Doll Cereal, a short-lived product that had marshmallow Barbie icons like cars, hearts, and diaphragms. (Well, two out of three.) ANYWAY . . . at the end of the commercial, the little girls who were having breakfast

with Barbie had to go to school. When they
waved good-bye, they said, "Bye, Barbie! Bye,
Barbie!" At the presentation, I joked with the
client that I had put that in for subliminal rea-
sons. What kids would hear subliminally is
"BUY Barbie, BUY Barbie."*

Admittedly, the thought that we are being subliminally persuaded to do something can be a little chilling. AND . . . this subliminal nature of indirectness is why some men get bugged out by women who give indirections. When/if a man realizes postdeed that a woman indirectly got him to take a certain action, he feels annoyed/resentful/nervous/fearful of this woman—and future women who may have this effect on him in times to come.

I'm not the first to point out that many men find women mysterious witchlike creatures because they cannot fully understand our beguiling powers. These powers can be scary to a man, so he reaches for negative adjectives like "manipulative" or "shifty" to describe a woman whom he feels has power over him. Interestingly, "manipulative" and "shifty" are also how the Japanese are often described, suggesting a bit of poor sportsmanship on businessmen's part.

BUT BACK TO THE WOMAN ANGLE ON THIS . . . It's odd how disturbed men can be by a woman's indirectness. HENCE . . . the expression "femme fatale" was born.**

But our indirectness is not anything manipulative or shifty or dark or evil or witchlike. Our indirectness—and I hope you don't mind if I

---

*NOTE: But I was only joking when I said this to the client. Really. It was there for liter-
ary reasons, as the crucial climactic ending to my thirty-second story line.
**NOTE: I find it intriguing that we women don't have the analogous male lingo at our
disposal: homme fatal.

speak for all of us here—has nothing to do with that. It was created by a combo of empathy for others and fear of others.

Deborah Tannen even defended indirectness as not being a purposefully manipulative act when she said:

> "[Being indirect is] no more manipulative than asking 'Is Rachel there?' and expecting whoever's there to put Rachel on the phone. Only a child would answer yes and continue holding the phone."

The above directive is simply a softer version of saying "Put Rachel on!" which, in contrast, can sound stern and off-putting, and thereby create less good will between you and the person on the other end of the phone—or the other end of the conference table, if you talk in a similarly harsh, direct fashion during a meeting.

Remember, kindness and sensitivity are valuable attributes for continued success—as Daniel Goleman noted in his book *Emotional Intelligence*, and as G. K. Chesterton implied when he said:

> "The reasons angels can fly, is that they take themselves so lightly."

Your business flight will go better if you take yourself lightly. Though being light can be hard. As Hakuin said:

> "Should you require the great tranquility, be prepared to sweat beads."

But before you go get your sweat suit and Gatorade, consider . . .

THERE ARE DISADVANTAGES TO THIS FEMALE ADVANTAGE

$\mathcal{I}$ didn't want to mention this too soon and spoil our celebration of being as talented as Japanese businessmen, but being indirect can get us businesswomen into trouble, too—AND the same kind of trouble the Japanese can find themselves in.

The Japanese speak a different language, which often is mistranslated. Ditto for women.

For instance, many times when a woman says:

"I don't care."

She means . . .

"HOWEVER, if you cared, you could read my mind."

Don't let yourself be a martyr in a situation. If someone isn't doing what you told them to do, it could be because you communicated indirectly and they didn't hear your directive underneath your niceties. So we women must be sure to repeat ourselves more clearly until we feel we're understood. And try not to get miffed. Remember, even successful Japanese businessmen have this same problem with men: miscommunication due to different languages.

The Japanese know not to take it personally. Too many women, however, do. I believe this is why so many men think so many women are crazy. In fact, every time a guy says a girl is crazy, I always wonder what he did to contribute to making her crazy. Usually her "craziness" is inspired by some mutual miscommunication.

A Common Symbolic Example
A woman says: "Do I look fat in this dress?"
indirectly making a plea for a man to tell her:

*"Not only do you look amazingly vixenlike,
but Kate Moss is waaaay too skinny."*

*Instead, a man responds with: "Yeah, yeah, the
dress is great."*

*His meaning: "Come on, come on. Hurry up,
we're late for the party."*

*Her response: "You mean I look fat, don't
you?"*

*His response: "No. Look, I told you, we've got
to go!"*

*The result: Women and men see each other as
nuts and dolts.*

We women must learn to be more direct. Often very direct. As
Machiavelli said:

*"[A leader should] appear merciful, faithful,
humane, religious, upright, and to be so, but
with a mind so framed that should you require
not to be so, you may be able and know how to
change to the opposite."*

MEANING . . . We women should learn how to feel comfortable
being both "stern at times" and "benevolent at times," to be a balance of
both, a nice bad girl—or a bad nice girl.

Just like there are good witches and bad witches, there are good
bitches and bad bitches. Be a good bitch. A good bitch knows when to
use her powers—and uses them in the fight for good, not evil.

Staremaster

For Indirections

1. When you ask a question and want a positive response, shake your head "yes" as you wait for the reply. A subliminal plus.
2. Don't disagree, even when you disagree. For example, say: "I agree with you that this coffee we're drinking is really bad, and that's exactly why I like it. And why you should like it. Because it's different from the gourmet coffee that everyone is now serving. Being different is good. So you're right. This coffee is good."
3. Sun Tzu recommends that if you are going to do battle with someone, do the opposite of what they expect you to do. For example, if you think they think you're going to do a hard sell with a directive, then be soft—or vice versa. MEANING: (1) You'll catch them off guard, (2) they won't know what you're really thinking, (3) you'll have more power. BUT keep in mind: How you trick them, you, too, can be tricked. As the Tao says: "One must be a fox in order to recognize traps, and a lion to frighten off wolves." Which reminds me of another point. If someone asks you to do something that you REALLY think is NOT appropriate, tell them "NO" clearly and directly. If you can't do it as clearly "as a lion," then do it as "a fax." No, that was not a typo. I meant fax. Fax 'em a direct letter if you can't say NO out loud.
4. Be aware of how many directives you give. Don't overload people with assignments. Remember: Working with others should be a give-and-take thing—and that doesn't mean that *they* give and *you* take. You should both be symmetrically and symbiotically helping each other.

2

MOMMY MOMENTUM

*W*e women are innately more nurturing than men—and lucky us, we can use this propensity on clients and fellow employees. Particularly childish, misbehaving clients and fellow employees. Which is A LOT of clients and fellow employees.

Interestingly, psychologists say that for the first few years of childhood the actual definition of the word *mommy* is NOT literally "mommy." More specifically . . .

Mommy = I need love

It's not until years later that . . .

Mommy = mommy

Then, a few years after that . . .

Mommy = you've ruined my life

But that's *another* book to be written.

Which reminds me of a book *already* written. Child psychologists had a surprisingly positive reaction to *How to Make Your Man Behave in*

21 Days or Less, Using the Secrets of Professional Dog Trainers. They believed most of my dog/man-training tricks also applied to child rearing. One of the main principles shared between the two is motivating behavioral change through love. The dog/man/child will want to behave better when a warm, loving bond is firmly established. Ditto for clients and fellow employees.

Lucky us, we women reflexively nurture and empathize with those who are quarrelsome or contentious, giving women an advantage over men at the office. It's like this . . .

> *A woman instinctively motivates behaviorial change through:* **warmth.**

> *A man instinctively attempts this through:* **war.**

Men instinctively deal with adverse behavior head on, with authoritative directives. In a family setting, this results in kids who wind up feeling:

> *Father knows best*
> *BUT*
> *Mommy is loved best.*

Meaning:

> *Daddy might be bigger, brawnier, brawlier,*
> *brazenier, brashier*
> *BUT*
> *Mommy silently rules.*

After all, love is one of *theee* most highly potent forces. It's been known to empower ordinary folks with godlike strength that enables them to lift a car off a trapped loved one. And a car is even heavier than one of my suitcases packed for a weekend Berkshires jaunt—and I dare anybody to try to lift one of those babies.

My Point

If love can give people the strength to lift cars,
it can give them the strength to lift a phone to
make an important work call or lift a pile of
reports off a desk to be sent out to the appro-
priate clients.

My Point in One Quick Sentence

Love conquers all—even laziness.

My Point as It Relates to Women
(i.e., YOU)

Because corporations share an interactive hier-
archical infrastructure—just like a family—
women can silently rule with their innate
mommy-nurturing skills here as well.

All of the above points are very much true—but admittedly with
one catch. We women must make sure we use Good Mommy Skills and
don't become:

Bossie Dearest
or
Employee Dearest

You know the type I mean, I'm sure. Who knows, maybe YOU are
even the type. Though I hope for your sake, and your blood pressure's
sake, and your coworkers' blood pressure's sake, that you are not. This
type can best be described through the following story:

A Past-Life Repression

Back in my advertising days, I had a "Bossie
Dearest" (hereafter called B.D.). B.D. mostly
spoke in capital letters. Meaning B.D. SPOKE
LIKE THIS ALL THE TIME! B.D. was very
much into punishment. Meaning B.D. would say
stuff like: "IF YOU DON'T FINISH ALL THE
WORK ON YOUR PLATE, YOU CAN'T GO OUT
AND PLAY THIS WEEKEND." And B.D. would
repeat this throughout the day without exagger-
ation ten times (and with exaggeration a hun-
dred times). Paradoxically, B.D. claimed to
want employees to be happy.

"I WANT THIS OFFICE TO FEEL LIKE A
FAMILY TO YOU!" B.D. once told me.

"Not to worry. It does," I responded, then
forgot to explain: My family is dysfunctional.

In the end, office productivity ebbed rather
than flowed. The only behavioral change B.D.
motivated was mass exodus. Which is one of the
cool perks of the office version of a family: You
can actually quit it.

B.D. was a control freak—a funny sort of people. Control freaks are
big fans of control when it comes to "control of others." But "self-con-
trol" is *another* story. If you have these tendencies at the office, it's
important you try to tame your out-of-control overly controlling ways. I
have a friend Robin who tried this, and said:

"I used to be a control freak. But now I'm in
control of being too much in control."

It took us a moment before we realized the humorous contradictions in finding a cure for being a control freak. But with the skill of will you can—and a lot of office life demands you should.

The mommy skills I want to recommend are obviously *Good Mommy Skills.* They apply to the positive, nurturing caretaking of BOTH:

1. Employees *(if you're a Good Mommy Boss)*
2. Projects and coworkers *(if you're a Good Mommy Employee)*

Let's begin with . . .

1. GOOD MOMMY BOSS ADVANTAGES

a. A Good Mommy Boss (hereafter called a GMB) instinctively gives her employees enough carefree playtime to enjoy, knowing that all work and no play makes Jack want to draw mean-spirited cartoons of you in various torture modes instead of writing up that important report due on Monday morning. ALSO, whenever possible, a GMB joins in the playtime. She takes breaks from her busy schedule to lally around with employees at that office playground called the watercooler and to celebrate birthdays and big career hurdles with a good party.

b. A GMB follows her own advice. If she doesn't want employees to arrive late, *she* does *not* arrive late. She recognizes that "visual aids" help in teaching. Eventually . . .

> *One's actions* convince *louder than one's words.*

c. A GMB knows not to do everything for her employees, but to let them learn how to do things on their own. She instinctively wants her employees to grow up independent, resourceful, and cling-free, knowing, as that famous saying goes:

*"Give a man a fish, feed him for a day.
Teach a man to fish, feed him for life."*

Not only does a GMB teach her employees how to fish, but afterward, she DOES NOT hover over their fishing poles. She gives them space, thereby showing her trust, thereby instilling confidence—knowing as Hodding Carter once said:

*"There are only two lasting bequests we can
hope to give our children. One of these is
roots; the other, wings."*

A GMB also knows it takes time to learn. You gotta crawl before you go Rollerblading. So a GMB knows to . . .

*Encourage
to help give
courage*

d. A GMB recognizes that a misbehaving employee (e.g., one who never does his homework on time or leaves his metaphorical dirty laundry strewn around) is acting out aggressions from a subconscious—or even conscious—angry place. Rather than fight aggression with aggression, she visits this place.

This Visit Is a 3-Stop Journey to
1. *A listening place*—taking time to really hear an employee's complaints.
2. *A validating place*—acknowledging an employee's right to their perspective, and trying to actually see it along with them if possible.
3. *A responding place*—together, working to come up with a satisfying solution for all involved.

A wise GMB even acknowledges that rebelliousness can be a positive sign—one that signals an independent thinker with backbone.

MEANING often it is the rebellious kid/employee who is "the most likely to grow up fastest." A GMB wisely and generously offers this individual special tutoring, which includes:

1. The GMB is sure to point out specific examples of behavioral problems rather than just making sweeping criticisms like "You're not being a team player."
2. The GMB explains how a misbehavior blocks reaching the end goal. The GMB highlights the importance of the end goal.
3. The GMB practices tough love, meaning she's stern about misbehavior but sets up a safe environment in which to talk things over by practicing unconditional and nonjudgmental acceptance.
4. The GMB not only punishes/ignores misbehavior, but rewards good behavior.

E. A GMB recognizes sibling rivalry. For instance, a new addition to the family might create jealousy—and the unwillingness to share one's toys (e.g., computers or fax machines). The GMB watches that she doesn't play favorites. She knows that calling a new employee a cutesy name that signifies favoritism (like "Senior Vice President") might make an old employee pout a bit. A GMB makes sure she cares for any bruised egos *immediately* so they don't get worse.

2. GOOD MOMMY EMPLOYEE ADVANTAGES

a. A Good Mommy Employee (hereafter called a GME) recognizes that giving birth to an important work project is *a lot* like giving birth to a child. And ONLY we privileged women are entitled to these pregnancy lessons to better prepare us for work challenges to come. REMEMBER . . . Men *can't* sign up for these Pregnancy Lessons—lessons that teach valuable stuff at a visceral level. Consider for yourself . . .

What Giving Birth to Work Projects
and Kids Have in Common

It takes time. Months and months. Then you're
never prepared when the real due date hits.
Meanwhile, during these months of prepara-
tion, you get nauseous a lot—in between pig-
outs. If it's a really difficult project, you gain a
lot of weight and don't feel like having sex.
THEN THERE'S LABOR PAIN. I believe if a
woman can put up with labor pain, she can put
up with anything *in the labor force. (Though*
there are also some *jobs that will make labor*
pain go easier.) ANYWAY . . . Lamaze helps
both kinds of labor pain. Breathe, breathe,
breathe. It relaxes. It relieves. It helps to focus
you on the end goal: what you are giving birth
to and how much you want it. Another big les-
son: Enjoy the journey—these unborns are
born and grow up all too quickly. *

b. A GME realizes that she can learn a lot from the projects she's
raising—especially the unruly ones. She learns about her personal
strengths, her weaknesses, her priorities, her passions. A GME doesn't
get lost in the ordeal; she finds her true self in it. A GME acknowledges
what Eric Fromm said:

"Man's main task in life is to give birth to
himself."

*NOTE: All of the above is helpful for us "single unwed nonmothers," (as I jokingly refer
to us unmarried chicks, due to society's disappointment in us for not mating up) . . . ANY-
WAY, my point is that due to the above similarities, we can test out the ol' embryonic
waters with that "baby surrogate" called "a project" to see if we even want to have kids.

Same goes for a woman's main task. In other words:

Go knock yourself out with work, then knock
yourself up. Give birth to your Highest Self.

c. A GME recognizes that raising a project can be exhausting. Usually when the project is most rambunctious and out of control is when it most needs a nap. A GME gives the project and herself this break. Try to find a way to take a catnap—even if it is just to put your head down on your desk for fifteen minutes.* You'll be amazed what a difference it will make.

d. A GME has read all the books on child rearing and understands some of the . . .

Tricks of the Mommy Trade as Applied to Coworkers and Clients

1. If you're going to give a kid a choice between two things, *remember* that he'll almost always pick the second thing because he hears it last. A GME can use this to her advantage by asking her boss, "Would you like me to have this report ready for you on Tuesday or would you rather give me a paid vacation?"

2. If you want a child to go to bed, don't ask him if he wants to. Imply that he will by posing questions like "Do you want the lights on or off?" A GME can do this to set up appointments. Instead of asking "Can we set up a meeting?" say "I can meet you either Wednesday morning or Friday afternoon."

3. If a child is not doing what you want, distract him with a toy—or a tickle. A GME can use this in meetings. Change the subject with a joke or a lighter topic, then return to the subject when the coworker seems more receptive.

---

*NOTE: Be sure to make certain your office door is closed.

But before you start stocking up on Dr. Spock and Erma Bombeck, consider ...

THERE ARE DISADVANTAGES TO THIS FEMALE ADVANTAGE

*G*ood Mommy Bosses can sometimes wind up with the menial tasks. MEANING ... While men are busy cleaning up in the monetary sense, women are busy cleaning up in the Cinderella sense. All too often, a Good Mommy Boss can get sidetracked helping others with trivial pursuits, while men forge ahead—and forage the monetary bonuses. And all too often, nurturing can be misinterpreted and/or just plain be a bad trait. In other words:

> *When we aim to please, we can wind up with bad aim.*

As Gracián said:

> *"Don't belong so much to others that you stop belonging to yourself. . . . He who gives too much doesn't give; he sells. Don't exhaust the gratitude of others. When grateful people are unable to respond they break off the correspondence."*

It's sort of like those guys who wash your windshield at the stoplight. You didn't ask them to wash it, but there they are—and then they want something in return. So make sure when you give, it's not with guilt attached.

IN GENERAL: Make sure you're not the kind of mommy who's into guilt.

Staremaster
For Building Up Good Mommy Momentum

1. You can tell a lot about how a person will interact with her coworkers at the office by learning about her childhood. Many of us have what I call a "Portable Childhood," which allows us to set up our childhood-learned dynamics wherever we go. For instance, if someone had a problem with authority figures in her childhood, chances are it will show up in the office. So it's helpful to find out a bit about your officemates' childhood so you can be prepared for the dynamics that inevitably will ensue. Also, be careful not to play out *your* "Portable Childhood" at the office.

2. Here's a message from my own modern version of a *Primer for Career Gals*:

   "See Dick. See Jane. See Dick tell Jane that
   there are no day-care options or good pregnancy
   leave opportunities for Jane at this company. See
   Dick be one. See Jane band together with other
   women—and men—and try to create change.
   Go, Jane, go!"

3. Actually, the untying of all those marital knots this country is witnessing is in the long run good news for businesswomen. As divorce rates rise, so does men's awareness of the need for improved day-care options. By dividing parental care into "your weekend/my weekend," men are becoming better educated about what it's like to be a mommy, and thereby gaining more mommy empathy—and in particular more *working mommy* empathy, since most of these dads are working dads.

4. As the song goes: Baby, You Can Drive My Karma. Helping,

nurturing, and having compassion for others comes back to you in the end in the form of success.

5. Advances in fertility drugs are good news for women. We can better control our biological clock's alarm, ensuring it doesn't go off at an inconvenient time in our career schedule. You should be sure to mention this to any chauvinistic employer/client/coworker/assistant who questions whether your maternal instincts will interfere with your career commitment. Plus you can remind them that "Home is where the PC is." The advent of home computers and fax machines now enables women, both with and without children, to work for a company from home. Even start a company at home.

6. My mother's not the only mother who is using guilt to her advantage this decade. Mother Nature is, too. We mistreated her, and now she's rebelling and demanding that we make it up to her. We're seeing greater environmental awareness in the product arena. And we women, with our innate mother nature instincts, can help keep our corporate conscience clean, along with our sky and water.

7. Have men noticed yet that one of the major services they had to offer us women when it comes to parenting is now obsolete? I'm talking about how men no longer must go hunting for meat. Back in caveman times, it made sense for women to be the ones to stay home with the kids, since men were better built to chase down wild boars and other "fast food" dinner entrées. Now that men and women are equals at capturing animals, due to this invention called "a supermarket"—and another invention called "Chinese food delivery." Since men and women are equals at bringing home the bacon (or the lox, depending upon your preference), there's no reason why women must be the ones to remain at home with the kids.

3

VERBAL ESSENCE

$\mathcal{A}$ woman is innately more verbal than a man. In fact, according to scientific research, we girls are *born* to talk:

> *"Females are earliest to develop finesse in language, logical thinking and fine motor coordination, while males excel in math and are better oriented in three dimensional spatial relations."*

MEANING . . . if you're a typical girl, and you just read the above paragraph (compliments of *The Brain* by Time-Life Books), chances are you innately grasped its meaning more deeply and quickly than a typical guy.

These verbal differences are due to our brains' differences. Men are more controlled by their right brains, while women are more controlled by their left brains—*and* have more interaction between the two hemispheres than men.

Language is a left-hemisphere function, which means we left-brained girls get to reap the benefits of advanced speaking skills and higher scores on verbal tests. Right-brained guys, however, also get a benefit from their right-hemisphere predominance: greater incidence of left-handedness. If you ask me, though, we females decidedly lucked out in this left brain/right brain deal.

                Women get: *better communication skills*

and

                men get: *to use those funky left-handed scissors.*

No insult intended. I think lefties are great people (which I guess is the ultimate left-handed compliment). However, thanks to two new societal trends, we women have the upper hand over the average left-hander:

Two New Societal Trends That Favor Women
1. The Internet
2. Time scarcity

First let's take a look at . . .

1. **The Internet:** It's rapidly becoming a predominant part of our culture, especially at the office. Many businesses are finding that communicating through E-mail saves time and money. The more active business becomes on the Internet, the more at an advantage we verbally oriented women will find ourselves, for five biological reasons:

Women's Brains Give Women
1. Innately superior spelling skills
2. Innately superior vocabulary skills
3. Innately superior typing skills
4. Innately superior reading skills
5. Innately superior shopping skills (which, it seems, is a major direction in which the Internet is heading, by briskly becoming an electronic shopping mall—women will feel right at home).

2. **Time scarcity:** In this time-scarce society, superior verbal proficiency has an ever-increasing value—even a literal value, as those who own cellular phones will *especially* attest.*

Even beyond the cellular phone benefits, verbal proficiency is a valuable skill to have or look for in others (a major e.g.: those lawyer-others—who charge college tuition rates by the hour). If you can communicate clearly the first time around, you can save yourself some extra rounds, AND . . .

The Two Most Precious Resources for Success

1. TIME
2. ENERGY

Advertising was a good training ground for learning how to speed up whatever outgoing messages I needed to send at meetings, and in memos and reports, not only because it was a fast-paced business but because I was being trained to write thirty-second TV commercials, which translates into the art of the thirty-second sales pitch. In seventy words or less I had to:

GET YOUR ATTENTION

EXCITE YOU

QUELL YOUR DOUBTS

PERSUADE YOU TO DESIRE, DESIRE, DESIRE

CREATE A CALL TO ACTION**

*NOTE: A cellular phone, with its outrageously exorbitant rates, is an effective training device for any of you eager to learn how to speak more pithily and to the point. The less you speak, the less you pay. What better incentive is there?

**All of this while getting you to forget about those tasty SnackWell s cookies waiting for you if you leave the TV and head to the kitchen.

The ad business taught me quickly which words had value and which didn't. All businesses could benefit from the word *frugality,* because most people only remember sound bites anyway. In the last decade or so, politicians have caught on to this, and throughout their campaigns have . . .

Replaced
paragraphs of information
with
sound bites strung together

I recommend this—BUT ONLY IN MODERATION, or else you'll sound like a bad politician, instead of a highly intelligent, memorable, and vote-worthy politician.

Talking, however, is just one half of what proficient verbal communication is about. The other half of it is *listening*. At least it *should* be. As Fran Lebowitz joked in her book *Metropolitan Life*:

"The opposite of talking isn't listening.
The opposite of talking is waiting."

Sometimes we're so busy preparing in our heads that snappy comeback or persuasive argument that we don't fully hear what our co-conversationalist is saying. I believe men more than women suffer from this temporary deafness.

Many men, with their tendency to want to use conversation as an opportunity to instruct or problem-solve (as I mentioned earlier and Tannen has repeatedly mentioned), mistakenly view conversations NOT AS as an opportunity for

Dialogue,
BUT FOR
*dia*tribe *or* mono*logue*

NOT AS an opportunity to . . .

174

Discuss,
BUT TO
dis or cuss

This not only shows up at the office but at that other place that involves a lot of work and suffering: dates.

My girlfriend Lauren recently told me about a date she had where the guy wouldn't let her get a word in edgewise. At date's end, he ACTUALLY said:

> *"You are such a mystery to me.*
> *I know so precious little about you."*

I know: "Ugh." Right?

The office equivalent of this scene reaps more positive results for a woman. A man who chooses to offer so many of his ideas and opinions leaves himself open to be more vulnerable, because data—both business-wise and character-wise—can be collected and used to a woman's advantage in future interactions.

Another verbal difference between men and women according to Tannen is females are socialized in their youth to ask more questions, nod with interest, and interrupt less. All skills that:

increase *the coconversationalist's (or "cc's") comfort level*

increase *the cc's likelihood to reveal info*

increase *the cc's likelihood to reveal* revealing *info*

increase *the cc's interest in further dialogue*

increase *one's own popularity*

If one uses these conversation skills pragmatically with a client, it also may . . .

increase *one's money-making ability*

These same female socialization skills have ALSO trained us to instinctively follow one of Stephen Covey's seven tips for success. Covey advises in *The Seven Habits of Highly Effective People*:

> *"Seek first to* understand,
> *then to be* understood. "*

This strategy not only makes sense *emotionally* (because it helps the other person feel you *really* care), but *rationally* (because it helps you amass more clues about the other person's motivations, enabling you to gather the fodder needed to win the argument, make the deal, work compatibly with coworkers/bosses, etc.).

It's intriguing that women have such a reputation for talking so much, when so many of Tannen's studies prove that men do more talking. I believe that men have this perception because they think that conversational exchange for the sake of emotional exchange is frivolous and therefore verbose. Men don't value conversations about emotions the way women do.

HOWEVER, a woman's tendency to talk less can pay off more. MEANING, because a woman is frugal with her words, when she *does* speak up, her words potentially have more resonance, because they've been LESS diluted by an ongoing verbal influx. PLUS, a woman's words might have an added glow of credibility, since a less talkative person could appear as if she's hoarding her words until she *really, really* means them and needs them.

However, before you consider starting up your own 1-900-I-TALK-GOOD line, to profit from your verbal proficiency, consider . . .

THERE ARE DISADVANTAGES
TO THIS FEMALE ADVANTAGE

A woman definitely has an edge over men when it comes to discussions in small groups, but entering into larger group discussions or leading a group discussion can work like Kryptonite against a woman's verbal skills—a vulnerability left over from childhood. As I mentioned in Part 1, in our culture little boys are called on more in class, which leads to them believing in their opinions more, which leads to them raising their hands to talk more, which leads to them feeling okay about leading group discussions, which leads to them feeling okay about interrupting women during these group discussions, which leads to a woman's talking disorder during group discussions, or what I call "He Said, She Corrected Him, He Interrupted Her, She Whined, He Aggressively Countered, She Got Insecure Syndrome."

A major example of this from Tannen is how women turn their comments into inquiries.

> *What I mean is a woman poses her thoughts as*
> *a question, you know? Don't you agree?*

Or she accessorizes conversations with phrases like:

> *I'm not sure, but . . .*

and

> *Maybe...*

Plus, I find it intriguing that the first words I learn whenever I go to a foreign country are always:

> *I want*

The result:

I can say "I want" in seven different languages—except English.

Women must practice saying this phrase over and over. In fact, I WANT you to.

Another verbal flaw we women have: In our innate yearning to connect, we can reveal too much personal info. We need to keep in mind what H. F. Henrichs advised:

"The ancient sage who concocted the maxim 'know thyself' might have added 'don't tell anyone.'"

So be sure to keep a little personal mystery about yourself.

This rule also applies to maintaining a little business conundrum.* Be sure to reveal business information to clients on a "need-to-know" basis. As Gracián advises:

"Don't reveal too much—and keep them dependent on you."

Which, in a way, is the operating principle behind most male/female relationships. Men reveal less of the revealing stuff and innately feel most comfortable when they have set up a hierarchy wherein they are independent and women are dependent.

A woman has to get better acquainted with:

The Three Ups

WHEN TO PUT UP

WHEN TO SHUT UP

WHEN TO SPEAK UP

*NOTE: If the definition of that word is a mystery to you, then you're right.

178

These three ups go triply in meetings where you're trying to sell something to someone. Women who have a tendency for insecurity ALSO have a tendency to oversell. Once you've made the sale, remember to hold true to that crucial "second up": when to shut up.

Staremaster
For Increased Verbal Proficiency

1. REMEMBER to follow the advice my buddy Steve swears by:

   "Say what you mean, and mean what you say."

   After all, it doesn't matter how well you worded something, or convinced somebody with those artfully chosen words, if you cannot live up to them. If you *really* want people to pay attention to what you say, ALWAYS live up to what you say—or DON'T SAY IT.

2. Do an experiment. Try to have an entire conversation without talking about yourself. BAN all sentences beginning with "I." What does it feel like?

3. Take an improv acting class. It will help you loosen up around groups of people, give you some good pointers for being more spontaneous in meetings—and maybe help you over your stage fright so you'll feel more comfortable leading a meeting.

4. When you first meet someone, pay attention to the first three things that person tells you. These are things they consider priorities, and most likely will come up again and again in your business dealings with them. Obviously, the same goes for the first three things you say, so be aware of yourself as well.

5. Study your voice. Record yourself at a meeting or on the phone to see if you suffer from too many "ums" or other conversational vulnerabilities. Then work on ridding yourself of them.

6. REMEMBER: Eye contact speaks louder than words.

7. Keep briefs brief. That's why they're called briefs. Make sure your first three paragraphs and last three paragraphs are your strongest—because this is all most people pay attention to anyway.

8. Tannen, in *Talking 9 to 5,* explained that because men and women talk with very different conversational rhythms, neither know if the other has completed a thought or is merely pausing between thoughts. Before you speak your mind with a man, wait a moment to make sure he is truly finished speaking. Similarly, we women should not let someone stop us mid–verbal stream. Many women are so used to being cut off, we've developed the habit of talking very quickly, which can make us seem insecure. So watch out that you don't end up sounding like that Federal Express spokesguy who talked at express train speed rather than at local speed. It's funny. I'm so used to being interrupted from my childhood dinner-table days, I've even joked that if I'm not interrupted when I'm talking, I worry that the other person isn't listening.

9. SOME TELEPHONE TIPS:

Telephone greetings: When you initiate a phone call, never launch into a conversation without up-front identification, i.e., your name (rank and serial number are optional).

Simultaneous phone activities: Also known as multi-tasking. People can sense when you are not paying 100 percent attention to them. Typing is especially rude because it can be heard over the phone. Eating while on the phone is *only* allowed if you select quiet foods like oatmeal, marshmallows, or Jell-O. Reading while on the phone is also *not* polite, unless, of course, we're talking about *this* book.

Cellular phones: Mostly, cellulars are as appealing as cellulite. Always have your phone nearby and keep the ringer on low. If you do get an incoming call and must interrupt the flow of a meeting or lunch, take the call in a private area, and return as quickly as possible. Remember, a telephone booth is a telephone booth. A restaurant and a museum and a bakery are a restaurant and a museum and an excellent place to buy temporary happiness.

10. And about that Internet . . . Basically, the same rules of regular ol' conversation apply on the net. No yelling, which means NO CAPITAL LETTERS. No obscenity, unless it's between two consenting adults—or one consenting adult and a consenting dog with really good typing skills.

4

FEARLESSNESS TO ADMIT TO BEING LOST AND ASK DIRECTIONS

*T*he fastest way to the corner office is to ask a straight line of questions that could help us get the right answers. Luckily for us women, we're not afraid to ask questions. Men, however, are. Wacky, I know.

Men Fear Not

KILLING LARGE, FURRY SPIDERS

RACING SMALL, EASILY CRUSHABLE CARS

EATING THAT FIVE-DAY-OLD PIZZA WITH ITS

MYSTERY PURPLE TOPPING — FOR BREAKFAST

Men Fear

ASKING QUESTIONS

Go figure.

Speaking of questions, here are a few to mull over:

What do you think would have happened had poor lost Dorothy from The Wizard of Oz *been a guy—say a "poor lost Donny"?*

ANSWER

Donny would have been singing:

> "I'm *following this* turquoise *brick road. No way am I gonna stop and ask a bunch of midgets directions.*"

In general, men prefer to follow . . .

The path of least assistance.

I find it ironic that men—a species that is afraid to ask a strange woman on the street directions—is *also* the same species not the least bit timid about yelling out to this same woman their private sexual fantasies.

Which is a "Go figure x 2."

Tannen also discusses how afraid men are to ask directions. One example she gives deals with a male pilot who could not admit he was lost and needed help, and therefore almost crashed his plane. For him, death was preferable to asking for directions. Comedienne Elayne Boosler has also discussed the potential dangers of Direction Phobia, joking that the reason Jews wandered lost in the desert for forty years was because Moses was afraid to stop and ask for directions.

Granted, at the office the repercussions of not asking for directions are not always this extreme. Rather than be lost for a full forty years, a man could be lost for only a week or two, until he finally figures out the "Aha!" of what his client meant—and then be forced to either rush to meet the client's goals or redo an inappropriately rendered report. Or a man could miss out on a crucial piece of information that could have triggered an innovative idea that might have boosted his career.

It's funny that men view Asking Questions as having questionable value. The way I see it . . .

Questions Are Good for You Because They Can

GET YOU ANSWERS — WHICH ARE GREAT TO HAVE AROUND

GET YOU EXTRA INFORMATION NOBODY ELSE AT THE OFFICE HAS

BE A PREVENTIVE WORK MEDICINE, HEADING OFF PROBLEMS BEFORE THEY DEVELOP

BE A CURATIVE WORK MEDICINE, HELPING ONE GET TO THE ROOT OF THE PROBLEM SO ONE CAN THEN PULL OUT THESE ROOTS

BE A SIGN OF AN INNOVATOR'S CURIOUS MIND AND THEREBY POTENTIALLY IMPRESS HIGHER-UPS

QUESTION #2

Considering the pros versus cons of questions, why don't men, with their "I ~~want to~~ *got to* be a winner" mentality, ask more of them?

ANSWER

It's that ego thing again, rearing its ugly swollen head. A lot of men believe that asking a question is proof that there is an exception to their omniscient powers. We women are less afraid of appearing vulnerable or in need of assistance. In fact, we view having someone help us as an opportunity to connect, bond, share with an empathetic, considerate person.

Women are also more familiar with this Information Exchange Program. Most of us surround ourselves with a group of female friends who serve this function on a daily basis. I have what I refer to as:

"The Girlfriend Board"

a.k.a.

"The Advice Squad"

Meaning . . . I'm always one telephone call away from getting the help I need. Male friendship cliques don't promote these same club benefits. A man could be going through a career crisis and choose not to "burden" his friends with the situation. For a man . . .

Asking advice = a vice.

This is why the Dear Abbys, Dear Heloises, and Martha Stewarts of this world appeal mostly to women. Conversely, men don't enjoy the hierarchal status of "the needing position." Men pride themselves on their independence. A popular musical score running through the movie of a guy's life is:

"I Did It My Way"

Receiving assistance means having to face some new music. PLUS . . . it also means one's boasting abilities must face a stumbling—and mumbling—block. Because . . .

$$Receiving\ assistance = \frac{a\ boast\ about\ a\ job\ well\ done}{2\ people\ having\ done\ job}$$

Instead of being able to say:

I did it myself.

A man might have to admit:

We did it myself.

Plus, for a man, Asking Questions not only means a momentary loss of independence but the long-term potential loss of another highly guarded commodity:

RESPECT

Respect is a biggie for a guy. *The Godfather* movies make a big point about this. A man who's "disrespected" could lose his head—or at least a nearby horse could.

A woman isn't as Respect Obsessed. She's more "love/help/I need answers" obsessed, so she will mainly see the advantages that questions offer—the same ones Sun Tzu saw when he said:

> *"If you cannot employ the locals as guides, you*
> *will not be able to obtain the advantages that*
> *the terrain has to offer."*

We women see and value the word

quest
in the word
question . . .

whereas men see greater value in the word:

conquest
and might be open to a
conquestion.

We've all seen examples of a man's comfort with "conquestions" (questions that lead to conquest). They usually occur in singles bars ("Are you free next Tuesday?") and interrogation rooms ("Where were you last Tuesday?").

QUESTION #3

Doesn't inquisitiveness show intelligence, not the opposite? (I asked ever so inquisitively.)

ANSWER

In youth, it's the child who asks a barrage of questions who is considered the smartest in the class—and eventually will become the smartest if given the right answers. If there are NO RIGHT answers, all the better. Parents revel in the spirited mind of a child who can stump them with unanswerable questions like:

"Mommy, why is grass green?"

Then, a few years later, update it to:

"Mommy, why is grass especially green on that other side?"

Unfortunately, as we grow older and older we notice less and less that there's an opportunity for a question to be asked. We tend to accept things, and even if a question does break through our fog of acceptance, we assume that because nobody else is asking it, the answer must be SO INCREDIBLY OBVIOUS we don't want to ask and potentially look silly.

But *this* is silly—as Alfred North Whitehead has contended:

"The silly question is the first intimation of some totally new development."

Alfred is right. For instance . . .

A Not-So-Silly Silly Question

Why is everybody standing in that long bank line, and nobody is standing over there, where

that teller seems to be open and alone? Hmmm,
nobody else is going into that obviously empty
line. There must be a reason. I guess I'll go
stand in that long bank line with everyone else.

The above circumstance is a good metaphor for a lot of missed business opportunities—a lot of "intimations of some totally new developments." Luckily for us businesswomen, we're less afraid of posing not-so-silly silly questions—for a similar reason a child might be:

A child

assumes he doesn't know an answer yet because he's new on this planet and is not yet a member of The Adult Club, who seem to know everything. For instance, if you'd never been to a bank before, you'd be more likely to ask about that bank line.

A woman

also assumes that since she's a new addition on the career scene, she might not know her way around the office as well as a guy, for whom business is socialized and automatically seems like more familiar territory.

A man

conversely feels as if he should have been born with a priori business acumen—knowing all business answers; therefore, he might be less likely to admit his birthright was slightly lacking.

QUESTION #4

Can one get ahead without questions?

No.

Next question.

Okay, okay, I'll elaborate a bit. You can*not* be a supreme success without being a risk taker, which means asking a lot of questions and not being afraid to look stupid—which probably wouldn't happen to you anyway, because if you *are* an innovative risk taker, you'd be likely to ask smart, challenging, impressive questions anyway.

Keep in mind that, ironically, it's the people who don't ask ANY questions who wind up looking the dumbest.

Or people who ask questions—but only really, really obvious, safe ones. When I was interviewed for *How to Make Your Man Behave* . . . , I could tell *a lot* about how smart an interviewer was by the questions he asked. Most interviewers asked the same obvious, safe questions—meaning, eventually, being interviewed became a no-brainer. Then every once in a while I'd meet an interviewer who was an innovator, a thinker, who would pose a question I'd never heard before—and I'd know this interviewer was on the path to great success.

There is, of course, an alternative to not asking a question to get an answer: trial and error. But this will only get you so far—and so fast. For instance . . .

CD Player from Hell

I bought a new CD player for my bedroom and thought I knew how to use it because I ALREADY owned a CD player. I plugged the new one in, turned it on, and was serenaded with a song—the same song—over and over and over. I assumed I knew how to fix it because I already owned a CD player—and therefore refused to seek the assistance of the instruc-

*tions. Twenty minutes—and one hundred
repeated serenades later—I sought the assistance of the instructions and finally realized I'd
inadvertently pressed the Repeat button.*

The above could be YOU at your office with office equipment—or worse, with an office problem—or worse, lots of office problems, with you doomed to face these same office problems over and over—and over and over—like that song I was serenaded with—or the movie *Groundhog Day: The Career Version*—until finally you break the cycle by seeking assistance.

Some Good News/Bad News

*The need to seek assistance will grow even
more important in the career marketplace of
the future. We are rapidly becoming a nation of
specialists. Jobs are splintering to serve very
specific purposes, meaning there will be more
and more need to go to one of these splinter
specialists for assistance with a list of
questions—which is a trend that is good news
for us question-friendly gals, and bad news for
the guys.*

But before you turn your next meeting into an episode of *The Firing Line* and wind up getting fired, consider . . .

THERE ARE DISADVANTAGES
TO THIS FEMALE ADVANTAGE

*A*s far as asking questions at the office goes, keep in mind:

> *You can ask some of the people, some of the*
> *time—but DON'T ask MOST of the people*
> *MOST of the time.*

Women can sometimes ask too many questions, and thereby appear as if they don't know what they're doing. Women must also be especially watchful of not asking too many of those goofy "Did I do okay? Did you like my report? Do I look fat?" questions. PLUS, we women also have another inquisitory tendency that works to our disadvantage: transforming what should be a confident statement into an insecure question. For example: "The marketing trend is *definitely* heading upward—uh, *don't you think?*"

One Question Never to Ask

Why me?

The Question to Ask Instead

How can I learn from this?

We women must keep in mind that the kind of question skills we *should* be honing are the ones that will get us access to career knowledge, not self-knowledge. The latter is another ball of waxing prosaic.

Remember

Self-knowledge is NOT to be found in the exter-
nal world BUT the internal world.

Another inquisitory tendency we women have to watch out for is that, due to our all-too-trusting nature, we can ask the right question BUT of the wrong person. We must learn to discriminate better and acknowledge that some people are not "safe" people to ask questions of. They could give an answer that's *misinformed* or *deformed,* due to either competitive reasons or brain-defective ones. So keep in mind who it is you're questioning, then listen to their answer with both ears—and both eyes—open.

A questionee might have one of five negative reactions to a questioner, which a woman should be prepared to handle:

Five Reactionary Reactions

1. The questionee might misjudge the intelligence level of the questioner. However, this usually means the questionee is insecure about asking questions herself—meaning she is insecure in general.
2. The questionee might be very busy with work and find the questioner to be an irritant of the gnat variety.
3. The questionee could overreact to the questioner's intent in asking the question by misinterpreting her as prying or overstepping boundaries.
4. The questionee could be competing with the questioner and will then know her area of weakness and later use it against her.
5. The questionee could give a brutally honest answer—one the questioner is not really ready to hear. So keep in mind:

The Rule Is

You can write the question, but you can't write the response.

Which leads me to two more pointers that inquiring minds might want to know.

A Reminder from Machiavelli

"A Prince must always seek advice. But he must do so when he wants to, not when others want him to; indeed, he must discourage everyone from tendering advice about anything unless it is asked for."

A Person Never to Question

Oneself

Staremaster
For Questions

1. If you want to ask a difficult question, ask a barrage of easy, harmless questions first, to get the person used to answering questions. Then, when the rhythm of the questions is set, slip in the difficult question.

2. In *What They Don't Teach You in Harvard Business School,* the author advises to play dumb sometimes. Ask a question to which you already know the answer, so you can test how smart or legitimate the other person is. Also, repeat your questions at a later time to test how consistent the answers are.

3. A good way to avoid answering a question you don't want to answer or don't know the answer to is to deflect it with another question. Check out the power of a "Why do you ask?" or "What do you mean by 'West Coast' demographics? Do you mean L.A. or all of the West Coast?"

4. When someone asks you a question, try to respond first with "That's a good question." It will make the person feel complimented and comfortable to ask you more questions. ALSO, it will inspire warm, fuzzy sentiments that maybe someday will result in this person offering up some top-secret answers to some of your questions.

5. You can pretend to answer a question by starting to answer it with "That's a good question. I was just thinking about that myself the other day." Then sneakily slip away on some tangent or cosine.

6. Although for the most part women feel comfortable asking for help, there is—as all rules have—an exception. Sometimes a woman can feel guilty for receiving assistance because she's so used to giving it. We must learn to feel secure in receiving from others, without feeling the need to immediately give something back.

7. Any questions? If so, write me c/o Harmony Books—and include a self-addressed stamped envelope and anything chocolate.

5

ADVANCED ROMANCE SKILLS

*Y*ou know all those secrets you've learned along the way for attracting and improving love relationships? They can be applied to improving work relationships, too, because love and work share boundless similarities.

I know, I know, at first glance love seems diametrically opposed to work. But then again, love is known to be a slippery, mysterious thing that's impossible to fathom, and as we know, love is *especially* slippery and mysterious at that first-glance stage. But there are, as I promised . . .

Boundless Similarities Between Love and Work

1. The search for a satisfying love or work relationship is as arduous and exasperating as the search for a lost contact lens—and equally as blurry sighted.
2. In work, this search requires a thing we call "interviewing." In love, we call it "dating." (Though I've been on many dates that have felt like interviews—and not nearly enough of the vice versa.)
3. Once found, both include LOTS OF demanding hours, white-lie

Band-Aids, getting screwed, kissing and making up, and fantasies about leaving, with the lure to remain around at least until Christmas —so we can get those terrific gift bonuses.

4. In a bad work relationship, we either quit or we're fired—but either way we ALWAYS MAINTAIN the "I quit" position. In bad love: same deal.

5. PLUS boundless more similarities—that's *with* exaggeration. *Without* exaggeration, another twelve—coming up in two pages.

But first, what's a theory without a few exceptions? So here's . . .

Two Dissimilarities Between Love and Work

1. Only one includes sex; the other doesn't. (Hopefully, you *already* know which is which.)

2. Only one pays you money for your troubles; the other doesn't. (Again, *hopefully* you know which one is which.)

By now you should be convinced that love and work are doppelgängers—and *glad* about it, because this is exceptionally *good news* for females. For most of us, love is an area of expertise. After all, it was not long after reading "Where's Waldo?" that we graduated to reading a new version of it in the form of "Where's Husband?" in women's magazines. These plentiful publications bombarded us with article after article teaching and preaching the art of seduction. HOWEVER . . . Neither a man's *Sports Illustrated* nor *Guns and Ammo* provide these services.

MEANING . . . you have learned a secret or two—or a thousand— about how to get the mate of your dreams that men have not learned, and you can apply all this wisdom to which you've been privy to getting the job of your dreams.

Let's begin with the number-one principle behind attraction: It cannot be rationally explained, but is dependent upon, as the French say:

A " je ne sais quoi" thing

Or as we Americans say:

game playing

Your attempt to attract your dream job can benefit from this very same game playing. A lot of you are now probably thinking: "Wait . . . Isn't, uh, isn't game playing a bad, bad, bad word?"

True—so let's not call it game playing. Let's call it "helping a desperate employer find the ultimate dream employee (YOU) who will transform their office into a little bit of paradise."*

TWELVE TIPS FOR ATTRACTING A MAN OR MANAGEMENT OF YOUR DREAMS

1. When looking for a job, use the sources you would for love openings: (1) Attend social functions, (2) take another look at past work relationships (what you turned down before could be right for you now), (3) ask friends and family—a BIGGIE. (I love watching movie credits, looking for Signs of Nepotism; often the last name of the director or lead actor is "coincidentally" the last name of the key grip or caterer, (4) talk to obscure folks like neighbors or friends of friends. Keep in mind:

   People who know people
   who know people
   who know people
   are the best kind of people
   in the world.

*NOTE: You can always comfort yourself with the cheery reminder that this potential employer is probably playing games with *you* about something.

2. Play hard to get. Never say "yes" to an interview without an audible flip through your calendar—and a twenty-four-hour lead time.

3. Jealousy works. Hint that others are interested in hiring you— be it true or not. You'll also notice that the best way to get a great job is to already have a great job. Just like with love, when you're not looking, everyone wants you.

4. Be confident—but don't oversell. REMEMBER, you're determining whether you want to buy what they're selling, just as much as you're selling yourself. If you believe this in your heart, you'll subliminally change the power dynamic of the interview. So talk less, listen more. Ask a lot of questions. Look around the place for clues—family photos, miniature-golf trophies, *Guns and Ammo* magazine. Ask about stuff. Let them talk. And talk. Determine whether you have THINKRONICITY. Would you want to see this person on a daily basis?

5. Ask friends if they've heard anything about how this employer has behaved in past work relationships.

6. When an employer asks about your past work relationships, try not to bad-mouth. In the end, the bad stuff you say will reflect more on you than on whom you're bad-mouthing.

7. Play hard to get when a job is offered. You'll set up a "you sure lucked out getting me" power dynamic that will last long into the work relationship—or at least until the honeymoon period ends. Speaking of honeymoon periods, THIS is when to ask for all those cash and prizes you want: when they're feeling the most desirous of you. So don't let them talk you into getting less now, more *later.* You may depart before later arrives.

8. Don't confuse a potential job offer with a real committed long-term job offer. Until/unless a committed proposal is offered, keep shopping.

9. Don't rush into taking the first job that comes along out of desperation. Speed kills—both in love and work. (I also don't recommend speed for dieting. I once tried speed to help me lose weight. All it did was make me eat faster.)

10. Get your beauty sleep before a big interview. Don't stay out late. (Don't arrive late either.)

11. Don't start doubting yourself. You'll find a job. Nature abhors a vacuum—almost as much as I abhor to vacuum. Keep in mind what Sogyal Rinpoche, Buddhist philosopher, said:

> *"I sometimes think that doubt is an even greater block to human evolution than desire or attachment."*

Or to quote another great spiritual leader, Doris Day:

> *"Que sera sera."*
> (which means, "Whatever happens, happens")

I don't know if her philosophy had anything to do with it, but wherever Doris was driving to, she always found a parking space out front. Optimism rewarded? Or just good timing? Who knows—but it does prompt a twelfth interview/dating tip:

12. REMEMBER, timing is everything.

Another romance advantage we have over men: Women are more commitment oriented, which can show up at the office as more job longevity and loyalty. Perhaps this commitment aspect of being female is due to our biologically proven longer long-distance vision being acted out in yet another aspect of our lives. Or perhaps it's simply because we allow ourselves to get more emotionally involved. Either way, this is an advantage we females offer employers that is often overlooked.

Putting a Contract Out on a Man

I once dated a guy who told me he was going to quit a senior position he had taken after months of negotiations and a mere three-week stint at the new office because something better had come along.

"Won't they be mad?" I asked. "Don't you have a contract?"

"No, I only have a commitment," he explained. "It's okay to break a commitment."

This was a scary comment to hear from him, considering that at the time he and I also had a commitment to each other. I had the sudden urge to ask him if we could get our relationship down in writing.*

As you can see, not only is romance work, but work is romance. AND . . . I'm sure you all have more love tips up your sleeves to make employers pant, but *first,* before you indulge in them, consider . . .

THERE ARE DISADVANTAGES TO THIS FEMALE ADVANTAGE

*B*ang, bang, bang.

That's the sound of me banging my head against the wall, a serenade that's been inspired by both kinds of relationships: love and work.

---

*You know what I find ironic? Men—a species that has trouble imagining where a relationship is going with a woman—is also the same species that has no trouble imagining a woman wearing nothing but red lace panties and spiked heels. Go figure.

The only thing harder than finding a relationship is *leaving* one. Women—more than men—not only take this "commitment" thing seriously, but *far too seriously.* REMEMBER:

> *In sickness and in health*
> *does* not *include*
> mental *sickness and health.*

All too often, women—more than men—remain in unhealthy, masochistic relationships (of both the work and love variety). Why? For a few reasons. Many women are operating under the . . .

Slot Machine Principle

> *I know I'm losing and have been losing for a*
> *while now here, but I've already invested SO*
> *MUCH, it's GOT TO hit big time any day now.*
> *Right?*
> *Right?*

Pink Elephant in the
Carnival Booth Principle

> *I'm refining my shooting skills, so I know I'll*
> *win that pink elephant any day now. Who cares*
> *that I've invested more than that pink elephant*
> *is actually worth? And who cares that I don't*
> *even need or want a pink elephant—or*
> *improved shooting skills? I've just got to win*
> *that pink elephant. I've got to. Right?*
> *Right?*

The Bad-Milk Principle

I remember how delicious this milk was when I first got it. It was soooo good. I know time has passed and it's soured a bit, but it was sooo good when I got it. I want it to taste that good again, and it will because it once did. Right? Right?

Basically what this is about is:

Fear of moving on

Which in many cases is the equivalent of:

Fear of not finding a new place to move on to

But if you've been unhappy for more than six months after trying to improve the situation, then I recommend making an appointment with your boss and breaking things off ASAP.

For the Record

Regardless of what the title of this book MAY imply, I do not recommend the Lorena Bobbitt approach to Breaking Things Off (she took that expression far too literally).

But before you move on, here's an important tip:

Learn stuff.

Figure out what went wrong so you don't repeat the pattern of your office life like some nightmarish Escher painting. Basically, a work (or love) relationship doesn't work out for three reasons:

1. **It's not you, it's THEM.** It's true. Your boss does suck. The situation sucks. Your friends agree. *Even* your *honest* friends

agree. However, they also agree that your complaints have the echo of familiarity. Your complaints about *this* boss remind them of your complaints about your *last* boss, meaning you're operating under . . .

The Lassie Principle

Every time Lassie died, they just replaced him with another Lassie.

You need to check out being with another kind of working dog—say a Beethoven. Or switch animals entirely. Check out working with a Babe or a Mr. Ed.

2. **It's not you, it's not them, IT'S SOMETHING ELSE ENTIRELY.** Maybe your office is downsizing—or sideways-sizing, meaning changing to incorporate a different focus—and you have to decide whether you like that focus (e.g., many advertising agencies are now focusing on direct marketing, the Internet, and PR). Or maybe the company is moving to a different location and you have to decide whether you want to make the move (e.g., the company might want you to move to a BIG city, and you're not sure BIG-city life is right for you).

3. **Heck, maybe IT IS YOU.** Maybe you need to change your behavior, or your attitude, or your deodorant—or your career path entirely. Maybe something very central needs changing. Ask your friends. Then ask your *honest* friends. Then ask your employer, if he hasn't already told you—as you were being fired. (Reread that pink slip and see if it mentions any name-brand deodorants.)

A Few Words About Being Fired

Being fired has a lot in common with being dumped by a lover: It hurts. Like a lot. It's a pain that's right up there with labor pain and bikini waxes. Thankfully, nature cleverly made us so eventually we don't recall past pain. Ultimately mothers willingly go on to give birth to second—even third—babies. And you will continue to seek new love, new jobs, and bikini waxes. In the meantime, try to see this as an opportunity to really *look inward. Often getting fired can be the powerful impetus needed to change what needs to be changed that you've been avoiding changing. In love, we lose those ten pounds. In work, we take those night classes. Try to use getting fired as your* satori— *a Buddhist word for "your moment of enlightenment." So when friends or future employers ask, you can tell them, "Me? I wasn't given notice. I was given a* satori.*"*

Staremaster
For Attracting the Job of Your Dreams

1. Remember: Everything should be done in moderation—including game playing. BUT holding true to my theory that all theories should have exceptions, the above moderation thing does indeed have one:

Smooching with Andy Garcia

And yes, "smooching" is a euphemism for "f——— all night like banshees." You know, banshees sure have it good. That's all they do is f———. I've never heard anyone say banshees do anything *except* f———. Nobody says: "I want to cook all night like banshees." Or "ski all weekend like banshees." Probably because banshees don't have the energy left to do *anything else*. After all, they've been f——— all night. AND WHO ARE THESE BANSHEES ANYWAY? What bars do they go to? Are any of them Jewish?

2. If you ARE a boss, you might want to familiarize yourself with the following two romantic lies to ease an interviewee's rejection pain:

   "If only I'd known about you six months ago."
   "I'll call you."

3. Jealousy can ALSO work against you. If your present employer finds out you're interviewing, he could become like a scorned lover. Try to be discreet.

4. My friend Sara said something interesting about love and work. She said, "When I'm at work, I'm thinking about my love life, and when I'm on a date, I'm thinking about my work life." I relate. And this is okay to do—however, once again, in *moderation*. But one thing to definitely watch out for is *talking* too much about your love life at work and *talking* too much about your work life on a date.

5. A super-good first interview and a super-good first date share the same potential problem: Love at first sight is myopic. So, *never* take a job without at least a second meeting with your employer, and ask to meet as many other people at the company as possible to get the full spectrum, in the same way you'd want to meet a potential boyfriend's friends.

6. The romance should not stop after the relationship begins. When you move into your office after accepting a job, make sure you set it up as a warm and comfortable place in which to hang out and have meetings. Consider an office makeover.

Marie Claire magazine recommended a book to consult for this, *The Office,* by Elisabeth Pelegrin Genel, featuring 250 photos of elegant work spaces.

7. One last romance/work tip: You know that expression "It's just as easy to love a rich man as it is to love a poor man"? I've re-written that as: "It's just as easy to complain about a rich man as it is to complain about a poor man." In the same way that you should never pick a man for his money, you should never pick a job for it, either. Pick a job for the same reasons you would pick your ideal mate: for what its soul is like, for its spirit. A work environment has just as much of a soul and spirit as a man does—in many cases, even more so than men. (I won't name names.) Anyway . . . look for a work relationship that offers all the important things of a love relationship: a sense of support, warmth, morality, and the opportunity for growth.

6

CLEAVAGE POWER

*M*any of you probably believe that a woman's cleavage can be a physical liability to her career. How on earth, you may wonder, can a man pay attention to what a woman is saying if he's lost in the valley of this doll? But that could be exactly *how* and *why* he *will* pay attention. Heck, a man will even pay *money* for a good cleavage viewing. Paying attention is at least cheaper than paying money.

MEANING . . . In certain situations, a little cleavage can actually help to first pique a guy's attention to a career girl's benefit—then later help to distract a guy's attention to a career girl's benefit.

IN OTHER WORDS . . .

> *A good push-up bra = a good* push-over *bra*.

Mae West, our nation's foremother of cleavage, once said:

> *"A curvy line is the loveliest distance between two points."*

I'd like to revise that to:

"A curvy line is the shortest *distance between two points."*

But I'm not just talking cleavage here. I'm talking the whole Female Sexual Object Package. This "package" can serve as a woman's power, not her powerlessness, if she knows how to wield it.

When a woman feels comfortable in her silky, smooth skin, she is more powerful in a general way that can benefit her at the office. For example:

How Taking Off My Clothes Got Me a Better Script Deal

I work from my apartment. One morning the phone rang while I was dripping wet from the shower and picking out what to wear for the day. It was a male MTV client on the phone, wanting to talk about my script rates. I negotiated with the guy while I sat wet and naked on my bed—a fact he was obviously oblivious to. But I was not oblivious to my nakedness. It made me feel, dare I say, sexy, powerful, provocative, wet, and wild. It was weird. I know it will sound weird, too, but I swear: Thanks to my nakedness, I DEMANDED MORE MONEY!

This story for me is about that *other* kind of female sexuality—the *raw stuff,* not the superficial goods. My MTV client never saw my superficial goods. That's not what got me more money. It happened because I was in touch with all that raw female sexual stuff.

MEANING . . . Repression of one's sexuality can be repression of a power that otherwise centrifuged could be quite a persuasive force.

MEANING . . .

YOU DON'T HAVE TO BE A SUPERMODEL.
YOU DON'T HAVE TO HAVE A D CUP SIZE.
YOU DON'T EVEN HAVE TO BE HETEROSEXUAL.

All you have to do is allow yourself to get in touch with every nook and cranny of your innate, God-given, and Goddess-given power—and that would, of course, include your *sexual* power. Don't repress it. The more at home you are in your body, the more at home you'll be in ALL CIRCUMSTANCES, including CAREER CIRCUMSTANCES.

The irony is: When a woman is totally secure in her sexuality, she can be the one who's sexually threatening to a man, rather than the man being sexually threatening to her. Because a sexually liberated woman is in control of her sexual power, a man may even be *afraid* to make a sexual advance on her.

So, if you're thinking "cleavage power" invites sexual harassment, think again. It could actually do the opposite: scare away sexual harassers, who are often turned on by overpowering the weak and timid, who they see as sexual prey rather than the bold and confident who they see as sexual predators. Plus, a man might subconsciously/consciously sense that a sexually bold woman might also be a *verbally* bold woman—one who might report a sexual harasser to higher-ups.

Sally Tisdale, author of the enlightening book *Talk Dirty to Me,* wrote about how men are often fearful of sexually liberated women. For example, a woman who works at Good Vibrations, a renowned adult toy store in San Francisco, explained to Tisdale that when men find out where she works they become "terrified" of her. She's even been told that she makes men feel "inadequate" because of the highly sexually charged nature of her work. She says, "If I don't tell men where I work, it's not because I'm afraid that they're going to grab at me. I'm afraid they're going to be afraid of *me.*"

In advertising, creative directors purposefully and wisely take advantage of all this potent female sexual power by investing billions of advertising dollars in using it in their ads—draping sexy women all over stereo equipment and cheeseburgers, knowing full well: Sex sells.

> SEX SELLS CARS.
> SEX SELLS CIGARETTES.
> SEX SELLS BEER.

My point?

SO . . . why shouldn't it also be true that:

> SEX SELLS A BUSINESS REPORT.
> SEX SELLS A BUSINESS DEAL.
> SEX SELLS A RAISE.

It's a logical deduction, isn't it?

AND BEST OF ALL . . . We women get to use this billion-dollar sales technique FOR FREE. No money down. So I say:

> *Let men have their penises!*

I say:

> *A cleavage can cut a penis down to size*
> *any day of the week!*

After all, a good cleavage (or even an average cleavage, for that matter) can control the mood a penis will be in—BUT it's not a vice-versa situation.

Even men who are paralyzed from their waists down have been known to get an erection in their phantom penis—*a nonworking penis*—if the right Female Sexual Object Package comes along. Now, *that's* some impressive power! I ask: Can a man beat that penis power—that is, the power we women have to move the otherwise unmovable?

I think a very persuasive, dangerous enemy to have—more so even than Khomeini—would be a *Khomeini with breasts*. Think about it. He could totally persuade his army to do *whatever* he told them—and maybe even some other armies, too. Trust me. Khomeini in a Wonderbra is a demagogue mankind should pray we'll never see.

But as far as womankind goes, all of this can be used to our benefit. I believe a Female Sexual Object Package can control both kinds of "staffs." That is . . .

> *A* staff *staff*

and

> *a* stiff *staff.*

I believe Sun Tzu was agreeing with me when he said:

"Weaken the enemy before engaging him, for his resistance can be thereby diminished before the engagement and you are in consequence strengthened. . . . Attack when he is unprepared, and take him by surprise. . . . Strike always with your own fullest strength against the enemy's weakest points."

MEANING . . . If a man believes a woman can be . . .

> *sexy or smart but not both,*

this is good news, because . . .

> *a woman* can *be sexy* and *smart.*

AND even better . . .

> *when a woman is sexy, a* man *is not always smart.*

IN OTHER WORDS . . . When in the presence of a sexy woman . . .

> *a man cannot see the forest for the bush.*

The result? A woman can surreptitiously take over a business meeting and persuade a man to make decisions and deals he may not otherwise be open to making. This is what my buddy David experienced when he was mugged by that woman/transvestite. And I believe this is what Sun Tzu was suggesting a woman do when he wrote:

> *"By employing diversionary tactics*
> *and keeping your real circumstances hidden*
> *you can fool the enemy in regard*
> *to your actual size and location, thereby forc-*
> *ing the enemy to spread out. . . . In this way the*
> *enemy's forces will be divided while your own*
> *remain concentrated."*

IN OTHER WORDS . . .

> *While a man is busy thinking about*
> *you* giving him head,
> *you can be* getting ahead.

But for the record let me state . . .

> *I* am not *recommending*
> *giving in to a boss's advances*
> *for career advancement.*

> *I* am *recommending*
> **flirting one's way to the top.**

> *I* am not *recommending*
> *sexually harassing men*

> *I* am *recommending*
> **a subtler sensual harassment kinda thing.**

Smile. Twinkle. Wear something that makes you feel beautiful and powerful. Everybody will benefit. You'll feel your best. And any man in your path will feel his best thanks to you, too. And people who feel their best are the most productive and generous—just the spirit a success-oriented woman wants to inspire.

But before you start thinking the right G-string will get you on C-Span, consider . . .

THERE ARE DISADVANTAGES TO THIS FEMALE ADVANTAGE

*I*n two words:

Anita Hill

Sexual harassment is a very real problem at the office. I know. Nearly all my girlfriends know. Nearly every woman I know knows. Because we have all experienced it to some degree.

FIRST-DEGREE SEXUAL HARASSMENT

This variety of sexual harassment is the obvious kind, like a direct sexual pass—though bizarrely enough, as obvious as this harassment might seem, it isn't always so obvious to the pass maker. For these folks I offer . . .

The Sexual Harassment Determinator

*It's not so unusual to be attracted to someone
with whom you work. And it's not so unusual to
want to express that attraction. Therefore, we
should all be allowed one polite mention of
appreciation for another's perky buttocks. This
is flirting. If there is no positive response, a
second mention is wasted flirting. A third*

mention is sexual harassment. (NOTE: See
Staremaster for defense against this offense.)

SECOND-DEGREE SEXUAL HARASSMENT

This variety of sexual harassment is seemingly innocuous—for instance, during the O.J. trial reporters often mentioned Marcia Clark's lovely figure, without ever noting how cute O.J.'s defense team's buns were. Unlike a successful man, a successful woman who is attractive will always get noted for how attractive she is. If she has a great figure, her body could receive more attention than her body of work. This constant appearance-rating commentary has long-term effects on a woman's sense of self. It can mess with her priorities, values, and how she chooses to spend her time and thoughts. The result?

Women experience "pretty" as an adjective.

Whereas . . .

Men experience "pretty" as an adverb.

MEANING . . . Men are culturally conditioned to view themselves first as:

PRETTY TALENTED

PRETTY SMART

PRETTY FILTHY RICH

WHEREAS . . . Women are culturally conditioned to view themselves first as:

Pretty

or

pretty not pretty

In *The Beauty Myth,* Naomi Wolf wrote about beauty and the beast of burden it can be for us women as a result of our cultural upbringing. One of the big differences we women encounter are the slew of self-improvement products pitched us: wrinkle creams, cellulite creams, bikini waxes, douches, mustache-bleaching kits, cosmetics, and diet aids, to name just a few things cluttering our bathroom cabinets and our psyches with the reminder:

YOU ARE IMPERFECT JUST THE WAY
YOU ARE.

Because men aren't marketed such an abundance of self-improvement paraphernalia, they aren't reminded of their imperfections as frequently as women are. I find it ironic, too, that men, a twice-as-sweaty bunch than women, are pitched half as many hygiene products. And why are women marketed painful procedures for hair removal—i.e., waxing and electrolysis—but men, who are far hairier, are not?

All of the above questions lead to:

a woman who questions her appearance

Which leads to:

a woman who won't feel comfortable cashing in
on the power of her appearance

Which leads to:

a woman a man can control more and thereby
fear less.

This, my friends, is why some men have problems with women in the first place. They fear a woman's sexual power—a power that overpowers their sense of control. Look at Donald Trump, a man of great power, rendered puppylike around Marla's maples. Men know: A woman who's comfortable with her sexuality can disempower a man.

Thus, it seems men have tried to disempower women first through the insecurity-inducing messages they send us from Madison Avenue and Hollywood.

Silicone implants are also an effective way to defuse the power of women's sexuality. Breast implants result in less sensitive breasts, thereby the lessening of a woman's arousal level. By deactivating a woman's sexuality, you create a less-threatening woman, one with less desire to cheat or seduce. Then throw in the perk of perky breasts, and *voilà,* you've got the ideal woman!*

It seems that no matter what a woman looks like, her appearance can get her into trouble.

Not-so-attractive woman: LESS ATTENTION FROM MEN.

Attractive woman: MORE ATTENTION FROM MEN, BUT WITH FEAR AND RESENTMENT.

Then there's a woman's response to another woman's appearance. Many women can feel even more threatened than men by an attractive woman, which I'll discuss further in Part 4, "It's a Cat-Eat-Cat World."

So, what does all this mean for us women?

The best advice I can give is don't try too hard to be something you are not. If you become overly self-conscious of what you are wearing or looking like, then you will lose focus of your Career Waldo. So be yourself at the office—but your career self. Don't be your party-girl self.

---

*NOTE: What I want to see is an operation that increases a woman's sexual pleasure, not her breast size.

Staremaster

For Getting the Right Kind—and Right Amount—of Stares at the Office

1. The first time you're being sexually harassed, you can try to make light of things with a joke, like, "Anybody ever tell you that you do a wonderful imitation of Clarence Thomas?" Even though, as you know, I am a fan of humor, I admit much of sexual harassment is nothing to joke about, and in these serious cases, I suggest the following actions:

   a. Be absolutely direct about your disapproval of his language/touching you. Warn him that you will take legal action if he is ever offensive again.

   b. Keep a new and separate journal of his offensive behavior.

   c. Find out your company's grievance procedure—and be aware that once you start talking about the harasser with your higher-ups, you will be questioned in detail. Bring your journal. Also know that by reporting the harasser you might find out that others have complained about him, which will strengthen your fight— and help these women to strengthen their fight, as well.

   d. If you feel your company is not being proactive or empathetic, report the situation to the EEOC. Be aware: If you want to file a complaint there, you must do it within 180 days of the harasser's initial harassment.

   e. If things continue to get worse without getting better, get yourself a lawyer who specializes in sexual harassment. Be aware, though, that these cases are difficult to prove, and emotionally draining—still, you will be helping other women at your office by letting the harasser and other potential harassers know they cannot get away with this unacceptable behavior.

2. In the movie *Working Girl,* Melanie Griffith plays a secretary on the rise who says, "I got a head for business and a bod for sin." This dynamic duo is a good one to hone, so try to do a little Nautilus for both the head and bod every day. Read the relevant business publications for a minimum of twenty minutes, and work out or do yoga for a minimum of twenty minutes. The workouts will give you a triple benefit, by invigorating that body, mind, and spirit triumverate. You'll release stress and thereby be able to think more clearly and have more energy to apply all those clear thoughts to action.*

3. A woman can benefit from faking orgasm at the office—meaning pleasure under the most tiring circumstances. Ironically, businesswomen can learn from the ultimate representation of femalehood: Miss America. Smile, smile, smile. Never let them know how tight your shoes are—or how tight a spot you're in.

*Plus you'll be able to wear Donna Karan suits.

7

WIDER OPENNESS TO CRITICISM

I once went to a psychic who told me, "You are a perfectionist."

"No I'm not," I answered. "I'm not nearly a perfectionist enough."

Although it sounded like a joke, I meant it seriously. I can always find fault in whatever I am presently doing. Like the above few sentences. I have revised them already *twice,* and will revise them again before this book is done—or even edit them out entirely so you might never have to read any of this. In fact, I just decided I'm going to edit out the entire next paragraph. . . .

ANYWAY . . . My point is: It's not just me. We women are constantly looking inward at ourselves and our lives. We are full-time explorers on a journey through inner space. I don't know if it's a genetic-makeup thing, but it is definitely a generic makeup thing. Consider the concept of makeup: a product created to correct faults in one's appearance. The message in each bottle: You are imperfect and need to change.

In one of my past lives (1988–1995), I freelanced as an image consultant for L'Oreal and Revlon, creating names for products like lipsticks. Some of my suggestions: Pinkorrigible and Pleasantly Plum. Though some more-to-the-point names might have been: Lips N'otsensualenough Stick or Eyes Too-Small Liner.

We women, myself included, buy this stuff because we buy into the concept that we need to try harder to improve ourselves—more than men buy into this. Think about it: ONLY women are sold makeup, NOT men. Some might say it's a:

Chicken/Egg Thing

We women are CONSTANTLY being pitched cos-
metics in magazines and on TV, so our confidence
about our appearance EVENTUALLY becomes
frailer than men's and therefore we start to think
we need to buy makeup, so we buy it, so we are
then continually pitched makeup. . . .

Though it could be a:

Chick/Ego Thing

We chicks buy makeup in the first place
because our egos are frailer TO BEGIN WITH,
due to childhood programming.

Little boys are bred to have more fortified egos, whereas girls grow up more receptive to believing criticism about their appearance and a checklist of other neuroses. It goes back to that Worrier/Warrior Difference. Tell a guy his business presentation in the client meeting wasn't up to par, and he'll forget about it five minutes later and move on to the next thing. Tell a woman her report on the Miller Account was not complete, and she'll review her report, ask three people to read it, and work on it until it is perfect. Eventually, women become more practiced

at self-analysis (and self-blame). This is why women—more than men
—read:

Self-help books

Men would probably want to read—if they existed:

Other-people-need-help books

But all this is GOOD BUSINESS NEWS for women. An excess of
male ego can stunt business growth because it shuts out criticism—one
of the main sources for learning the necessary lessons that lead to
growth and success.

We women are highly receptive to self-improvement. That's why
you are reading this book—and what motivated me to write it.
Personally, I want to *always* be learning new improved ways to improve
my life. Writing this book has been that for me.

We women love to spend time exploring our inner world. We get
turned on by pursuing an . . .

inner course

almost as much as men get turned on by pursuing . . .

intercourse.

We women instinctively recognize that making mistakes and receiving criticism are opportunities for growth, so we're more receptive to
these "opportunities." As I mentioned earlier, our childhood programming
also familiarized us with receiving more criticism than men, so this familiarity helps the medicine go down.

There's a hidden irony in criticism, too. You know those folks at the
office who are the most critical of you and whom you therefore perceive
to be hostile and not your friends? Well, they are the very same folks
who will help you learn the stuff you need to learn to rise to the top—
faster even than your warm and complimentary friends. As Gracián
pointed out:

"Flattery is fiercer than hatred, for hatred corrects the faults flattery had disguised."

For this reason, don't avoid the criticism of your foes and faux-friends. Listen with an open mind. These people don't care whether you like them or not, so they can afford to be honest. However, many men, more than women, will choose to block unsought criticism, adopting the "Mr. I'm Right" position, thereby losing out.

Granted, not all criticism is worth taking. Perhaps even *my own* at times, dare I say. So be sure to refine your sassing-out skills. Consider the motives for criticism. Jealousy—as well as subconscious jealousy—are often at play. I once heard an expression (I forget where):

Those who can't create destroy.

That explains a lot of the negative commentary from account executives, film/art/music critics, and inane/insane bosses.

Another inspiration for criticism is repressed personal issues. For example:

Remember O.J.?*

When O.J. was a twenty-four-hour-a-day ordeal,
I was subjected to various opinions on the case.
"What bugs me about this whole situation is
how the victims, Nicole and Ron, are being
ignored—their pain, their suffering is being
ignored," said my recently divorced friend.
"The case is about lying, how this whole coun-
try lies to serve their interests or get into the
spotlight," said my L.A. agent friend. *"It's*
about how the rich can get away with any-

---

*NOTE: I hope there will be a time when someone will answer "Who's O.J.?"

thing—even murder," said my struggling-artist friend. *"It's about how wife abuse is ignored in this country,"* said my feminist friend. *"It's obviously all a race thing,"* said a black friend.

Keep in mind that when people offer criticism, you get a petri dish full of their personal issues with it. So swallow criticisms with caution.

Another advantage women have when it comes to criticism: We know how to give it better than guys. I don't mean to criticize the way some men criticize, BUT some can criticize too harshly. For example:

"That's the stupidest thing I ever heard.
Men don't know how to criticize! How idiotic!"

Or men can criticize too arrogantly. For example:

The Story of H

A few years back, I took a creative writing class. When my teacher handed me back my corrected paper, one of the things he'd corrected was how I spelled my name. He had crossed out the "h" in it: Salmansohn. I couldn't believe his arrogance. I teased him: "Oh my God, I can't believe I spelled my last name wrong. Wait till I tell my parents! They've been spelling it wrong for years!"

We women have better criticism skills, because we tend to have better empathy skills; most women instinctively begin with a little praise session before the critique session hits, helping to soften blows to the ego. The only criticism about this way of criticism is that a not-so-astute employee might *not* hear the criticism part, *only* the praise. So we women, to be sure, should always ask the other person to repeat back what *they think* we've been rambling about.

But before you start asking for second and third opinions of your latest office project, keep in mind first that . . .

THERE ARE DISADVANTAGES TO THIS FEMALE ADVANTAGE

*W*e live in a society that is heading toward giving more and more and more opinions/critiques. Both the advertising and movie industries have what is called:

Focus groups

This is a means by which advertisements or movies are analyzed (which is a euphemism for "picked apart") by a sampling of the demographic group the creative people wish to please. The collected commentary is then used to make adjustments to the advertisement or movie. The result?

Painting in Numbers:

Imagine Picasso had painted with the help of a committee:

Committee Member #1: Hey, Pablo, why is that girl's nose bent like that?

Committee Member #2: And what's she doing with three eyes? I never saw a girl with three eyes. She's not very attractive.

Committee Member #3: Yeah. He's right. Maybe it shouldn't be a girl!

Committee Member #4: Hey, why don't you make it a painting of the committee president's son?

Committee Members 1–3: Great idea!

Picasso had balls to paint the way he did. (Balls "cubed," some might say.) Had his work been subjected to a committee's feedback, his balls would have been history, and he would not be in history.

Many folks subscribe to the belief that:

Suffering aids creativity.

I disagree. I'm most creative when I'm happy. HOWEVER, I do believe that:

Creativity leads to suffering.

As Ayn Rand said:

"Man has been taught that it is a virtue to
agree with others. But the creator is the man
who disagrees."

Innovators must face a lot of criticism. Not only do they have to wrestle with their own inner demons, but with those outer demons, too. This double wrestling match can be quite exhausting. But to succeed is to risk and to risk is to face criticism. As Ayn Rand also said:

"All your life you have heard yourself
denounced not *for your faults, but for your*
greatest virtues. You have been hated not for
your mistakes, but for your achievements. . . .
You have been called selfish for your courage
of acting on your own judgment and bearing
sole responsibility for your own life. You have
been called arrogant for your independent
mind. You have been called cruel for your
unyielding integrity. You have been called anti-
social for the vision that made you venture

upon undiscovered roads. . . . You have been
called greedy for the magnificence of your
power to create wealth."

Or to sum all of that up in a mere six and a half words:

"You're nobody until somebody hates you."

Unfortunately . . .

Women hate to be hated.

Chances are we will be hated if we're doing our job right. And if we're doing our job "rightest," we most definitely will be. Rather than face dissent, a woman might become too open to the criticism she receives and wimpily change a project or an opinion to please others, not sticking to her guns—and her intuition.

MEANING . . . If someone tells you that what you're doing cannot be done (TRANSLATION: That's not how I would do it or how I have seen it done before), then this is usually (but not always) a sign that you're thinking like an innovator, a leader, a success-oriented person.

ALSO KEEP IN MIND . . . Indifference can be stronger criticism than actual criticism. It means you stirred ZERO reaction. In fact, if you really want to insult an innovator-type personality, call him average.

"You, you average *person, you!"*

. . . is a much worse insult to an innovator-type than:

"I despise your work!"

We've all heard this philosophy before, but worded as:

"There is no such thing as bad PR."

Any PR agent will agree. It doesn't matter what's being said as long as *something's* being said. Machiavelli agreed with this, then added another level to it:

"An able prince should cunningly foster some opposition to himself so that by overcoming it, he can enhance his own stature."

In the Hollywood scheme of things, this is called "having a comeback from a dead-end movie career." And it makes the success all the sweeter—and the PR all the greater. Which brings to mind that aforementioned mantra:

John Travolta

Which brings to mind another two words/one mantra:

Christopher Columbus

Had this world cruise director been too receptive to criticism, where would we be today? I know I personally wouldn't be ordering up Chinese food from my apartment here in Manhattan. I also know I would not be here right now writing this book had I listened to all the criticism I've received in my life, beginning with:

*YOU SHOULD PICK AN EASIER CAREER
THAN ADVERTISING.*

to

*THAT WILD AD YOU WROTE WILL NEVER
FLY.*

to

*AFTER WRITING ALL THOSE WILD ADS YOU
GOT AWARDS FOR, YOU SHOULDN'T QUIT
YOUR SUCCESSFUL AD CAREER TO
WRITE A BOOK.*

to

*YOU CAN WRITE A BOOK, BUT DON'T
WRITE A BOOK THAT COMPARES
MEN TO DOGS.*

to
WHAT'S WITH YOUR HAIR?
YOU NEED A HAIRCUT.

Success requires knowing when to listen to the right criticism to the right degree—a skill that can be honed by honing one's self-esteem. A woman with healthy self-esteem realizes what the Buddhists have recognized:

> *No one outside ourselves can rule us inwardly.*
> *When we know this, we become free.*

This includes your mother. Even my mother. Even Einstein's mother, who also doubted him at times—specifically those times he was blamed for blowing up laboratories.

Speaking of blame, another problem some women face in the face of criticism is taking the blame for everything.

> That miscommunication: *my fault.*

> The car breaking down on the way to the
> meeting: *my fault.*

> Bosnia: *my fault.*

> The San Andreas: *my fault.*

Men don't overly apologize. For a man, love of money often means never having to say "I'm sorry." (More often it's "*You'll* be sorry!")

Women can benefit from their openness to accept blame—just be careful you don't hog the blame credit. If you do feel the urgency to apologize, do it once, then SHUT UP ABOUT IT ALREADY. As the Buddhists says:

> *"If we do not let go of fire with our hands, we*
> *cannot avoid being burned."*

This also includes not torturing yourself silently about a criticism for too long. Give yourself a forty-eight-hour statute of limitations on feeling stupid about a mistake.

Wayne Dyer told Deepak Chopra that every time he gets a negative thought he tells himself, "Next!" I recommend this—or reminding yourself how lucky you are to have learned something new to benefit your career.

Self-criticism also comes packaged as a thing we call "perfectionism." Although we may rationalize perfectionism as the desire for self-improvement, sometimes it exists for other reasons. As a perfectionist, I have, of course, perfected the art of rationalizing my rationalization of my perfectionism—in other words, I've explained to my agent, Lydia, how my second novel is still not completed because it's gaining new layers of depth and texture. Lydia, however, has come back with two alternate realities to consider:

1. It's not complete out of *fear of success.*
2. It's not complete out of *fear of failure.*

She's not sure which one it is, but she's more inclined to believe my perfectionism is rooted in the fear category.

And to perform any action out of fear is to operate from an area of weakness—not strength—and strength is the position where the perfectionist is more inclined to believe she is operating from.

Perfectionism/self-criticism that is rooted in this negative emotion of fear is a big-time energy dissipater, expending your energy without moving you forward. It's the equivalent of keeping your foot on the gas pedal while your car is stuck in a sand dune, so the wheels spin round and round and round, but you stay put.

So be aware if you keep changing and rechanging and re-re-re-changing a report, so that it never leaves your desk, that your perfectionism/self-criticism may not be about seeking the forward movement of the quality of the report—or forwarding your career.

Staremaster
For Criticism

1. REMEMBER, the more risks you take, the more mistakes you will make—which hopefully means you'll be making lots of these mistakes. Rename them in your head as "risktakes." Think of them as nobly as a soldier thinks of his Purple Hearts. Make a list of them in your journal and write about what you learned from each.

2. Don't ask too many people their opinions, or you might wind up with too many opinions. I always thought "focus groups" should be called "unfocus groups" because so many opinions can be confusing. ALSO, don't show your work to someone before it's finished. Chances are, in your head you are filling in the blanks that the other person does not see. Their negative comments could then diminish your enthusiasm and confidence.

3. Accept it: You will be criticized this year. Maybe even this week. Maybe even in an hour. We are human. We humans make mistakes. I told my boyfriend Josh at the beginning of our relationship, "I'm sorry." He asked, "For what?" Which was a good question to ask because I had not done anything. I explained that I wanted to give him an "I'm sorry" coupon now while I was so blissfully in love with him and everything was so wonderful and perfect because I knew at some point I would do something stupid to piss him off because I am human and now, while I'm in bliss with him, I know that I should apologize and I figured I might not have that clarity of mind later. Sure enough, a few months later we had a fight and you can be sure he asked to cash in my "I'm sorry" coupon.

8

THE EMPRESS' TAILOR

*S*ome folks say that women are too obsessed with clothes. This upsets me, because, well . . . it makes me nervous about how these folks got access to my American Express card bills.

I admit it. I love beautiful clothes. Rather than fight the lure of this superficial passion, I have, as I've done with superficial passions past and present (e.g., Cappuccino Commotion and Andy Garcia), developed some wonderful rationalizations for it.

RATIONALIZATION #1
FOR LOVING BEAUTIFUL CLOTHES

Manhattan is a city with few trees, few flowers, few natural sights of beauty. With so little natural beauty available, we Manhattanites must make do with what we have available, and surround ourselves with beauty where we can. I do this through Donna Karan clothes.

This rationalization has worked very well for me, but in case you don't live in a big city and need a different rationalization, I've got an even stronger one—one that relates to succeeding in business.

RATIONALIZATION #2
FOR LOVING BEAUTIFUL CLOTHES

A woman's heightened wardrobe awareness can serve her powerfully in business. We women grew up—as I mentioned—earning an honorary master's in clothes and packaging, which men don't have. This degree comes in especially handy here in the nineties—a.k.a. "The Age of Packaging," where style often supersedes, or at least distracts from, content.

Chances are you've probably already noticed how style is now playing the lead part in the success of movies, while content is cast aside to a mere supporting role. We're being bombarded by a slew of slacker films that should be renamed *slicker* films, and commercial films that are just that: *commercial* films—as in ninety-minute commercials. Personally, I will forever remember:

The Prince of Tides

as

That Movie About Streisand's Long Fingernails

and

Godfather 3

as

That Movie About Andy Garcia Looking Sexy in That Black Leather Blazer

(in two words: yum yum).

Here's a little Media Trivia: When I was a creative consultant for MTV and VH-1, I was amused by how I often dealt with larger budgets for creating the promotional campaigns for a TV program than the producers dealt with to create the actual TV program.

I suppose this shouldn't be so surprising, considering we live in an era where even someone who attains a dignified position like president of the United States is subjected to schoolyard insults about his tubby tummy or goofy haircut. Think about it. Clinton gains a little weight, and that carries the weight of front-page-news status. Imagine what the press would have said about those presidents of yore who were truly fat/crippled/plain dirt ugly. Though I suppose that in these image-obsessed nineties, they never would have been elected president in the first place.

MEANING . . . Good packaging is now not only CRUCIAL to the success of products, it goes ditto and double for humans. This is GOOD BUSINESS NEWS for women, because we have an advantage over men in knowing how to create the perfect image for ourselves and our work, thanks to childhood programming.

Face it. Here in the Age of Packaging, it's not just:

*Who you know and what you know, but what
you wear and how you wear it.* *

The omnipresence of TV and Hollywood seems to have hyperly heightened our visual sense and lessened our common sense, though human susceptibility to beautiful images has *always* been around. Ask Adam. He fell for the comely Eve's packaging. Trust me. It was not just the ripeness of that apple that sold him on eating it. It was Eve's ripeness. I don't care if all this happened BEFORE Adam was even aware of what nakedness was all about. That snake would have had a much harder time doing that apple sales pitch on Adam than Eve did.

---

*NOTE: And no, I'm not saying all this just to rationalize buying that new mocha-colored dress I saw at Bergdorf's.

Our language also reveals an ongoing attraction to attractive, superficial images. For example, we say:

>*It was love at first sight—*

not

>love at first sound.

We say:

>*We're seeing someone—*

not

>we're hearing someone.

You see what I mean?

Then there's that expression "see" what I mean.

Even Machiavelli recognized the power of packaging and the benefits of purchasing a good Armani suit when he said:

>*"Men judge generally more by the eye than by the*
>*hand, because it belongs to everybody to see you, to*
>*few to come in touch with you. Everyone sees what*
>*you appear to be, few really know who you are."*

Luckily for us women, we are well trained in the art of artifice, aware of the tricks of cosmetics and Wonderbras. And we are well read when it comes to the trade publications on packaging (e.g., *Mademoiselle, Cosmo,* and *Allure,* to name a few).

MEANING . . . We have attained higher educations than men about good packaging. MEANING . . . We women are less vulnerable to being fooled by packaging, and better prepared to do some major fooling ourselves.

Double-Agent Girl

>*Don't tell anybody, but . . . when I was working*
>*as a creative director in advertising, I was also*

*freelancing as a creative consultant for MTV on
the side. Whenever I knew I had to sneak out of
the ad agency during lunch to head over to
MTV for a meeting, I'd always pack a second
outfit in my bag—a sexier, hipper one, which I'd
slip on in the ladies' room before going to the
MTV meeting. At the ad agency I was expected
to dress "creatively"—but* not "outrageously
over the top better not scare our Phillip Morris
client with that million-dollar ad budget" *creatively—which was a very different "creatively"
from what MTV was looking for. I realized
ASAP that if I wanted to sell my ideas to MTV, I
needed to wear an "MTV player's uniform"—
one that wasn't so uniform. So I did. And I did.*

I definitely recommend that women dress for themselves—but a
self that is ALSO in keeping with their client's clothes. People prefer
people from their own "tribe." This is one of the reasons men prefer to
do business with men in the first place.

Suzy's Story

*My friend Suzy was nervous about meeting her
new female boss at this big dinner event. Suzy
of course dressed in a way she hoped would
make a good impression. It made a memorable
one. She arrived wearing THE SAME EXACT
outfit as her new boss. Suzy thought she'd die,
but later we discussed how this was actually a
positive sign, that she and her new boss might
share other things in common besides an
appreciation for Armani.*

Advertising taught me a lot about the hypnotic effects of good packaging—tricks that even *Mademoiselle* didn't teach me. Tricks that I'd love to share:

COLORS PLAY A PART IN GOOD PACKAGING

*D*ifferent colors have been proven to give off different vibrations that affect us on a subconscious, visceral level. That's why the color red is used on so many packages—it's been proven to stir an excited reaction in people. (In fact, red cars are known to be stopped more by policemen and, in general, have higher insurance rates.) Dr. Tessa Warschaw, noted psychotherapist and author, believes that "the color red has a physiological effect on the nervous system that stimulates blood pressure, respiration and heartbeat. Pure blue on the other hand depresses blood pressure, heartbeat and breathing. It has a soothing rather than exciting effect on us." Basically the rule is: Bright colors draw people out and inspire creativity; subdued colors relax people, making them feel less stressed. So dress according to the reaction you want to inspire.

PRICING PLAYS A PART IN GOOD PACKAGING

*M*any cosmetics companies package the same exact moisturizers and lipsticks at two different price levels. That expensive department-store brand you treat yourself to might be the exact same product as that cheaper pharmacy brand you look down upon. The price value affects the emotional value we project. This holds true for humans as products, too. When I worked at J. Walker Thompson, a female creative director gave me the wise advice to invest in highly expensive suits. When people see you dressed in expensive clothes, they associate you with success. They assume you're making money, so they listen more closely to what you have to say. This same philosophy applies to the pricing you give for salary or freelance fees. Raise them high, and your work will suddenly seem of higher quality. As I mentioned earlier, this worked for me as an ad creative director.

ESTABLISHED POSITIONING LIKE "BEEN AROUND SINCE 1876" PLAYS A PART IN GOOD PACKAGING

*I*t's hard to believe now, but there was a time when I wished I looked older. Back when I was in my early twenties, I sometimes had trouble getting attention at meetings because I looked so young. I had earned a place as a twenty-something senior vice-president, but many clients had trouble respecting my status because I didn't have enough wrinkles. There was one meeting I remember in particular. The client kept addressing my art director—an older guy, who reported to me. It bugged me that the client somehow could not grasp that I—a younger person, and a female person—was the head person on the account. I kept pretending I had a cough, to get the client's attention. I'd cough. The client would look at me. Then I'd speak. It worked. Soon after, I went to an eyeglasses store and bought a pair of fake eyeglasses I wore to all future meetings, hoping to look older and more established.

CELEBRITY ENDORSEMENT PLAYS A PART IN GOOD PACKAGING

*I*t helps to name-drop those people you know who are established and respected who support and believe in you and your work—but REMEMBER: Name-drop, don't name-downpour.

NICHE POSITIONING PLAYS A PART IN PACKAGING

*G*ood packaging of a product means unique packaging that stands out from the clutter on the shelf. Meaning, if everyone at your office wears red blazers, DON'T wear a red blazer. Wear a maroon one. You want to communicate to others that you are an individual who thinks differently from the crowd. I find it ironic that kids—eager to rebel and express their individuality—all wear nose rings, eyebrow rings, and low-riding jeans. The result? Everyone winds up all dressing in this outlandish way, so rather than be rebellious, they're homogeneous. In advertising, niche marketing means creating a point of difference that will separate you from the competition. The more unusual you are, the more you'll be remembered. A narrower focus will expand your potential hiring opportunities. Remember, it worked for me both as "A Swimming Cocktail Waitress" and as "A Writer of Funny Female Stuff." Even now, to enhance my niche positioning, I dress the part. I wear clothes that are feminine and a little outrageous, because this is how I write and think. It's a litmus test for clients. If a client is turned off, I save us both a lot of time, because chances are they would not feel comfortable with the outrageous direction in which I'd want to take a script.

SIZING PLAYS A PART IN GOOD PACKAGING

*S*mall, medium, large. Each size communicates a different personality. Same goes with humans. Tall men have been documented to have a business advantage when it comes to first impressions. But short guys have that Napoleon energy going for them in the long run. Me, I take no chances—and neither should you. I am only five foot three and a shmidge. I'm still waiting for my growth spurt. Unfortunately, I'm getting it, but in the wrong direction: horizontally, not vertically. But back to business. I always wear heels. Every inch helps. If a client is a lot taller than me, I make sure we spend more time sitting than standing.

Good packaging is key to success. But before you get out your American Express card, you can save yourself a few bucks if you consider . . .

THERE ARE DISADVANTAGES TO THIS FEMALE ADVANTAGE

*D*on't go overboard in the clothing department. In other words: You should not be investing more of your salary into your wardrobe than your retirement fund.

One of my favorite females, Coco Chanel, once said:

> *"If a woman is poorly dressed, you notice her*
> *dress. If a woman is impeccably dressed, you*
> *notice the woman."*

I agree and would like to add:

*"If a woman is overly dressed up, or always
wearing something new, new, new,
you notice her clothes* and not her, *too."*

MEANING . . . We women must resist becoming fashion junkies. Dress to express yourself, not the latest issue of *Mademoiselle*. Be aware of what the fashion industry is trying to tell us women—and why. In particular, right now there seems to be a trend toward demure pastels and baby-doll dresses. One might say this is a strategy to disempower women just as we're gaining power momentum. Be advised to dress:

less shy/demure

and

more confident/Demi Moore

Remember, too, that appearances can be deceiving:

*A Wonderbra is to breasts what a pinstripe suit
is to intelligence.*

Try to keep in mind the words of Hans Christian Andersen:

*"But the Emperor has nothing on at all!" cried
a little child.*

Here's yet another valuble Clothes Call to keep in mind:

A Zen Story

*This guy Ikkyu was invited to a banquet. He
arrived in schleppy beggar's robes and wasn't
allowed in. So Ikkyu went home, changed into a
fancy, brocaded ceremonial robe, and returned*

to the party. This time, Ikkyu was greeted at the
banquet with enthusiasm and warmth. His
response? He removed the robe and put it on
the chair, and said, "Here, I think this robe is
who you invited since you showed me out before
when I showed up without it." Then he left.

Be careful not to become a victim of this Age of Packaging. Make sure you're not spending more time concerned about what you're going to wear and how you look than the report or presentation you're going to make.

Don't start to believe your own hype.

Staremaster
For Packaging

1. This is also the Age of Phone calls, so be aware of your phone voice as part of your package. A large percentage of business deals are initiated or influenced by phone calls. Be sure to speak slowly, confidently, clearly. You might want to take voice lessons to get rid of a strong regional accent.

2. End meetings—and particularly interviews—with a memorable line so you leave them with something to remember, because usually it's the last thing said that's remembered. Studies show that in the movie focus group business, audiences will forgive a movie for a weak opening if it has a great ending. Even back in advertising, I wanted to position myself as "that swell funny writer," so I always tried to end interviews with a humorous comment. Once, at the end of an interview at the ad agency BBDO, the employer asked me: "Any questions?" I answered: "Yes, can you name all seven of the seven dwarfs? I believe you can tell a lot about a person by which dwarf they

241

name first and which ones they forget. Like if you remember Grumpy but forget Happy." A version of this story is in my novel *50% Off,* but it really happened. In real life, I got offered the job. I told this story recently to a new girlfriend. Her answer included a dwarf who didn't even exist—"Lucky," she said—which said a lot about my new girlfriend.

3. When I was a kid I couldn't decide whether I wanted to be a writer or an actress. Often I feel as if I got my wish to be both. Many meetings require all the skills of acting: the right costumes, the right staging, the right lines and expression of these lines. If I'm nervous before a meeting, I imagine how someone I respect would handle the meeting, then slip into the part of this person. Try it at your next meeting. Think of it as a performance. Imagine the person you think could handle the presentation, then play this part. Remember, all the world is a stage—so you might as well have the lead role on this stage. Don't settle for just playing a walk-on—or even worse, a tree in the background.

4. Another packaging advantage we women have over men: We know how to make things look nice. At home, we're superior at wrapping presents, knowing how to pick out the prettiest wrapping paper, the coolest and hippest ribbons, and making sure the tape doesn't jut out at the edges. At the office, this ability to "prettify a package" translates into a beautifully packaged report. We're superior at knowing how to choose the most appealing cover, a typeface that is elegant yet easy on the eyes, paper that is pristine yet strong enough to handle lots of flipping through, all of this adding up to a report that has the total look and feel of *Martha Stewart Meets Donald Trump.* And as we know, the medium is the message. So the better a woman is at creating an appealing medium, the more appealing her message will appear.

9

RIGHT BRAIN/
WRONG BRAIN

$\mathcal{W}$omen and men are called opposite sexes for good reason. We are very opposite. It's true: We women think differently than men, which is GOOD BUSINESS NEWS for us women. We get to have a totally different perspective on business operations, enabling us to see new business opportunities where men cannot. A woman has access to these advantageous contrasting perspectives for two reasons:

1. **Biologically:** Our brains are structured differently from men's, meaning our brains automatically see things more broadly.
2. **Sociologically:** Our collected life experiences are different from men's, meaning we learn to see things differently.

Let's cover that second one first.

Men, having lived many shared male life experiences, have a tendency to look at life from the same perspective. Same goes for women —with the exception of me and my friend Sharon within the last year.

Babies Versus Rabies

*Ever since my girlfriend Sharon started to want
to have a baby, everywhere she would go, that's
all she'd notice: babies.*

"Look at the adorable baby," she'd coo.

*"Where?" I'd say, not seeing a baby in sight
—because I'd be too busy looking at all the
adorable dogs.*

*"Did you see that adorable doggie?" I'd ask.
"What a beautiful doggie!"*

*Sharon's maternal instinct gives her height-
ened baby awareness and leads to more baby
sightings. Me, I am not yet feeling the maternal
itch—more like the "maternal bitch." Meaning, I
only notice babies when they are shrieking at
ear-piercing decibles in restaurants, and I am
wishing someone would give that baby a pacifier to calm it down—or me a pacifier, for that
matter. Right now in my life, I'm less maternal,
more dogternal. I notice dogs everywhere, not
babies.*

Eventually, I'm sure, the above scenario will change. Most likely,
due to my female programming, my focus will flip and all I'll see are
adorable itty-bitty babies everywhere, instead of cute doggie woggies
and shrieking, vomiting babies.

It's a nondebatable issue: When you are programmed to look for
something, you will tend to see that something more often. Hence, my
"Aardvark of Happiness Reprogramming Program." And hence how
men, who have grown up with many shared experiences, will tend to
experience the world and its "sightings" similarly—which could result

in viewing the business world in the same male-oriented way, with the same male-oriented "sightings."

Women, however, who have lived a different kind of life, with different kinds of "sightings," will look at business situations with what the Buddhists call "beginner's mind," a term I've mentioned earlier—and a term that's extremely positive, even though it has the word *beginner* in it.

In case you still have beginner's mind about beginner's mind, let me explain further.

There is a Zen saying:

The willow is green; flowers are red.

There is also another Zen saying:

The flower is not red, nor is the willow green.

Beginner's mind acknowledges that true wisdom means always keeping an open perspective to learning *and* unlearning—accepting that a closely guarded opinion could very well be wrong or only one of many. Beginner's mind is about seeing things for the first time—whether it is your first time or your 101st time—though of course it's always easiest to see things for the first time when it *is* your first time, which is a benefit we women have by holding a female perspective in an all-male boardroom.

For example, consider . . .

My Dad's Tollbooth Story

My dad and I were driving to Atlantic City together. We were coming up to the tollbooths when my dad, a stockbroker, said to me:

"You're about to see my theory on the stock-

*market. On the left are all the exact-change
lanes. On the right are all the lanes where you
need to get change. As you can see, most of the
cars are now getting into the exact-change lane
because they automatically assume it's faster
—therefore it's now more crowded and slower.
You'll notice I have exact change, but I'm getting into the lane where you need to get change
—the one thought to be slower, and therefore
it's the less crowded. And this, Karen, is also
my theory on investing in the stock market."*

My dad, who's not at all into Buddhism, didn't realize it, but he was ALSO explaining to me the concept of "beginner's mind." And because I believe a girl can never have too many tollbooth stories, here's yet another to further explain the benefits of beginner's mind:

My Tollbooth Story

*I was driving to my childhood home in
Philadelphia with my boyfriend Mark. Or, more
specifically, Mark was driving. As a resident
Manhattanite, I haven't had the need to drive a
car in years. The result? I have beginner's mind
about driving. I saw a sign that read:*
"SLOW DOWN, GET TICKET"
*Mark started slowing down. I got nervous.
"Don't slow down!" I warned him. "We could
get a ticket!"*
*When Mark realized I wasn't joking, he
laughed, then explained: The sign was in reference to the toll tickets being given at the tollbooth up ahead.*

Beginner's mind allowed me to read a new meaning into the sign that an experienced driver could not see. In business this could have resulted in a new perspective that could have led to $ or even $$.

Now, let's cover that first thing second: Biologically, men and women are as different as night and day or boy and girl. Even if we were raised exactly the same, we'd be different, because men's and women's brains are biologically/structurally different. Men's are bigger—15 percent larger. But as always . . .

Bigger on a man is not *necessarily better.*

Ned Herrmann, author of *The Creative Brain,* reported that in women's brains:

The Facts

"Neurons from one side of the brain travel to other side 5 to 10% faster than men's . . . [meaning] females can move ideas 'back and forth' faster than men."

The Translation

We women can process new information faster and perhaps better than men—because we're better equipped to relate new ideas to old ideas to make more new ideas.

According to the book *Brain Sex,* written by British authors Anne Moir (a Ph.D. in genetics) and David Jessel (a television writer and producer), who have researched brain gender differences for nearly two decades:

The Facts

*"Men tend to experience slight tunnel vision,
see a narrower field with greater concentration
of depth. Women take a bigger picture—their
wider peripheral vision is attributed to a
greater number of receptor rods and cones in
the retina."*

The Translation

*Women's brains are structured to see things
with a wider perspective, hence women might
make better long-range planners, while men
make good short-term-goal achievers. This is a
perspective held by Jayne Tear, president of
Jayne Tear Group, a consulting operation that
specializes in advising companies on how to
improve upon gender relations.*

Corrine Hutt, a British pioneer in the study of sex differences,
reported:

The Facts

*"Hierarchies and dominance are very impor-
tant to the male—perhaps because his brain is
structured to understand numerical standing
and spatial placement . . . [meaning a man
tends to view] the politics of power and the
measurement of success by numbers [e.g., dol-
lars]. . . . Competition, single-mindedness, and
comparison are all part of the spatially domi-
nant mind set . . . [therefore] for men winning*

is a concept easily understood . . . because it is
a way of . . . concretely measuring an outcome.
. . . For women the whole picture matters . . .
[because] her cognitive world is a lot larger."

The Translation

Males are more into numbers than females,
hence salary matters more to them. Males are
more into spatial relations, hence they're more
into ascertaining where they stand compared to
a competitor. Males are more rationally ori-
ented, whereas females are more emotionally
oriented, hence success for a guy includes
rational end results like: Win cash and prizes.
For a woman it includes emotional ends like:
Win friends and love.

Daniel Goleman, author of *Emotional Intelligence,* also believes
that . . .

The Facts

The emotional edge women have biologically
translates into a business edge. Goleman asserts
that one's business success can be made/unmade
depending upon one's people skills.

The Translation

Often what is seen as a

"*lucky*" *break*

. . . is really a

"friend in the right place" break.

Whereas a man might have the advantage of having more of these "friend in the right place" breaks due to his old-boy networking benefits, in time a woman's advanced emotional skills (stronger empathy, eye contact, and communicative talents) will help her to make more friends in more places and thereby eventually get more "breaks." With the passage of time, this could become especially true, considering that since men are less emotionally attuned, they might find that many of these "breaks" get broken.

Professor Howard Gardner at Harvard believes:

The Facts

There's more to intelligence than any single IQ test can measure. Besides the obvious sociological disadvantages that IQ tests subject different demographic groups to, Gardner believes intelligence should not be measured by one test, because intelligence comes in so many varieties—seven, to be exact—in which Gardner lists "Interpersonal Intelligence" as a valuable category unto itself.

The Translation

Conventional knowledge, like business statistics and product histories, can eventually be memorized and learned by both men and women alike. However, interpersonal knowledge, like empathy, cannot be taught. Either you got it or you don't. And it seems we women got it more than men got it.

Dr. Doreen Kimura, psychology professor at the University of Western Ontario, also reported:

The Facts

"Women perform better on tasks involving verbal skill or muscular coordination when estrogen levels are high (just before ovulation in the monthly menstrual cycle)."

The Translation

By being aware of this, we women can use it to our advantage. Time your next meeting or report around your ovulation, and reap the estrogen benefits. (NOTE: Kimura also speculated that guys might have a similar linking of fluctuations in cognitive skills with testosterone levels—levels that are higher in the morning than the evening. I guess this explains why my boyfriend Mark had what he called his "alarm cock." It also suggests that if you want to have a mental edge on a man, talk to him later in the day. He'll be a bit more mentally vulnerable.)

Right now if you're a woman you should be feeling pretty damn proud of your cerebellum, hippocampus, and basal ganglia, as well as all of—or at least a majority of—your brain's 100,000,000,000 cells and 1,000,000,000,000,000 connections, though you should also keep in mind about your mind that . . .

THERE ARE DISADVANTAGES
TO THIS FEMALE ADVANTAGE

*A*ll this brawny brainpower is of no use to you if you don't fully tap into it —and many of us women don't, because of those two enemies I mentioned in Part 1:

1. You
2. Everybody else

Let's cover the first one first.

Chuck Norris, world-champion martial-arts master, shared some of the secrets of his success in his book, *The Secret Power Within*. Norris wrote:

> *"Past a certain point, once you've mastered*
> *your art and brought yourself up to the peak of*
> *perfection, chances are each time you lose it's*
> *a result of the same problem: your mind."*

Norris explained how it is usually *not* lack of learned skills that brings defeat upon a martial artist but rather it is not being in control of one's emotions:

> *"No anger, pride, or overconfidence—nothing*
> *that will blur your vision—belongs in the ring."*

There's that clarity thing YET AGAIN, popping up to remind us how important it is to attain if you want to attain success. The ability to have emotional clarity is not just a luxury but a necessity for winning in "the ring" of any and all careers: the lawyer ring, the doctor ring, the accountant ring—even the author ring.

Right now you could be a veritable genius at your trade and it wouldn't be worth a penny of salary to an employer if you didn't know how to master keeping a clear head, even in the most stressful circumstances.

Correction

*That last sentence should have read: "**especially** in the most stressful circumstances."*

Because we women can be more emotional than men, we should be especially aware of Norris's advice on maintaining clarity during emotionally stressing times.

MEANING . . . We women should not be worrying about our intelligence keeping us back, or our education keeping us back, or our talent keeping us back, or our family life keeping us back. We should be worrying about our worrying keeping us back. I am referring to that worrier, not warrior, tendency I mentioned in Part 1.

We need to focus on our career goal and that Pep Talk we wrote about why we do very much deserve to achieve it. When we focus on our fears and insecurities, we *say things* out of fear and insecurity (which leads to others giving us fewer opportunities). And we *see things* that are all about fear and insecurity (which leads to us never leading anyone, but always following—and following that trodden road of negativity).

It seems I cannot repeat often enough: Negativity breeds more negativity.

A far too high percentage of women in this country are diagnosed with depression each year, and according to the book *Office Biology* by Edith Weiner and Arnold Braun, depressed people are 30 percent less efficient in learning—which can translate into a 30 percent career disadvantage, if you're not attentive to nurturing your emotional needs, and putting your emotional needs over the needs of others.

Although men display more of a warrior than a worrier disposition, their warrior side also has its negatives. Men must be watchful about their warrior proclivity to react with anger and aggression in emotionally stressful situations. Often that warrior bravura can provoke a man to venture into dangerous/difficult territories in which he is not fully trained to combat. These warrior predilections can blur a man's perspective and lead to him winding up facedown in the ring, instead of holding the winner's ring.

MEANING . . . Be you a man, a woman, or a child, you should be seeking clarity at all times.

MEANING . . . You should memorize the following simple yet powerful phrases:

> WAIT A MINUTE.
> HOLD ON.
> JUST A MOMENT.
> I'LL GET BACK TO YOU.

In emotionally stressful times, it's best to take the time to think things through. As I suggested earlier: Meditate in your office for five minutes, or take five minutes to write in your journal—or even reread your journal. Chances are your journal will eventually show you a pattern you have in dealing with difficult situations that you might want to reprogram yourself to avoid. All of these things, singularly or together, will help start those clarity balls rolling.

And speaking of balls rolling . . .

Nonbreakable/nonrollable balls are what you need to fight against enemy #2:

Everybody else.

The higher level of brain activity you use, the more opposition you will face from

1. People with less brain activity
2. People with the same high level of brain activity—but who are fearful

254

3. People with the same high level of brain activity—but who are competitive

All three kinds of people can make you feel insecure about your intelligence. Don't let them. Two things can help fight against them:

Balls

You need to use your balls to stick up for your brain. In metaphor land, your brain is the nerdy smart guy, and your balls are its bodyguards that protect you from being beaten up.

MEANING . . . Brainpower alone is not powerful enough. You need ball power to defend your brainpower. Here are some defense strategies.

1. When dealing with the first, "mentally challenged" variety of people, keep in mind what the Taoists say:

   "Great wisdom appears to be foolishness."

2. When dealing with the second, "taking ideas to new heights vertigo phobic" group of people, keep in mind:

My One-Inch Theory on Success

You have one inch to work within to be success-ful—in particular, at a corporation or a TV net-work. (Entrepreneurs, who don't need a higher-up's approval, might have a little more leeway—say, two to three inches.) When I recently presented a new TV show idea to a TV network, I confirmed my One-Inch Theory. I realized quickly that my TV show idea had to be just enough like an existing show so the TV net-work people could relate to it—but then, it couldn't be too much like an existing show, or

it wouldn't be fresh—so it had to be different—
but then again, it couldn't be soooo different as
to cause discomfort in a risk-adverse-
mortgage-to-pay-family-to-feed TV executive.

The Translation

I had one inch to work within.

3. When dealing with the third, "smart but unkind" kind of people, keep in mind one piece of advice:

   Fuck 'em.

   Oooops. Did I really say that?
   What I really meant to say was . . .
   Actually, I think that is what I meant to say.

Staremaster
For Brainpower

1. If you're presently in a job that requires delegating to others, keep in mind an important learning tip from advertising: You not only need "reach" (the target audience's attention), you need "frequency" (three exposures usually does the trick). In other words: Repetition helps learning. Which reminds me: Repetition helps learning. Which reminds me: Repetition helps learning. Which reminds me: Too much repetition is annoying/insulting, which can inhibit learning.

2. Another good learning tip: Use common senses—like sight, smell, touch, sound. The more of your senses you use when learning something new, the better. If you can see the info while you hear it—and even touch it in some way—your

256

odds of retaining this knowledge increases trifold. In *Office Biology* the authors even contend that if there's a smell in the room while you're learning something, a whiff of this smell later can help you retrieve the learned info. This holds true for other senses, too. The authors therefore suggest that it could be helpful to rehearse a meeting in the very room a meeting is to be held. Later, when the meeting is under way, the sight, smell, and feel of the room will trigger your rehearsal memories, and your meeting should benefit from the subliminal flashback.

3. Here are some foods for thoughts. According to *Office Biology,* some potent brain foods are: most B vitamins; vitamin C; the amino acids tyrosine and tryptophan; minerals like iron, copper, and zinc; and electrolytes like calcium, magnesium, potassium, and sodium. The popular "Smart Drug" pills on the market include many of the above—plus a caffeine kick.

   Ginseng is also supposed to help improve memory and brain functions, though basically, maintaining a good healthy diet and getting enough rest and exercise is probably the most powerful brain strengthener of all. (That's one of those "Duh, right?" things that we often forget.)

4. Become an expert in your field—then keep becoming an expert. Read, read, read. Talk to people, talk to people, talk to people.

5. Don't become *too* much of an expert. As the Buddhists say:

   "We do not need more knowledge, but more wisdom. Wisdom comes from our own attention."

   It's not just what you learn, it's knowing when and how to apply it—in other words, being aware of the specifics of what's going on at your office, knowing how to handle individual problems with their individual circumstances and individual individuals, and not attempting to solve all problems with generic memorized knowledge.

6. As I mentioned earlier, if you're in need of more clarity, check out meditation. Or yoga, even.

10

EVELYN WOOD PEOPLE READING SKILLS

We women speak and read fluent body language, faster and more accurately than men, enabling us to more readily understand the nuances of conversational subtext, ALL OF WHICH translates into a major power tool in negotiating, or even everyday business.

It's like this:

> WOMEN ARE MORE EMOTIONALLY ORIENTED.
> MEN ARE MORE RATIONALLY ORIENTED.*

This emotional edge makes women more innately in tune with people (innate people skills). MEANING . . . After a mere five minutes with a stranger, a woman could tell you what makes this stranger tick, what he had for breakfast—and what he wished he *hadn't had*. Basically, she could take this stranger apart piece by piece—then put him back together again.

Same goes with a man, only with a car engine, due to his innate rational thing-oriented skills.

*NOTE: With the exception of Rush Limbaugh and Newt Gingrich.

IN THE LONG RUN THIS MEANS ... At the office, men and women each offer different advantages:

Men

are better at fixing hard-to-handle Xerox and fax machines.

Women

are better at getting a fix *on hard-to-handle clients.*

Daniel Goleman, author of *Emotional Intelligence,* backs me up on this, explaining:

"The one rule of thumb used in communications research is that 90% or more of an emotional message is nonverbal."

MEANING ... Since women have been shown in studies to be more empathetic/intuitive than men, then 90 percent of the time women have an advantage at the office.

Peter Ouspensky says in his book *In Search of the Miraculous*:

"The subconscious mind functions at as much as 30,000 times the speed of your conscious mind."

MEANING ... Since we women are better at responding to others on a subconscious level, women have thirty thousand times the advantage over men at the office.

Okay, okay. I'm exaggerating, twisting statistics to suit my demented sense of humor, BUT women truly ARE more intuitive/empathetic than men, which CAN be a business bonus. Just ask Goleman, who says:

260

"[Studies/tests show] the benefits of being able
to read feelings from nonverbal cues included
being better adjusted emotionally, more popu-
lar, more outgoing, and—perhaps not surpris-
ingly—more sensitive. In general, women are
better than men at this kind of empathy."

After all, it's not what people say that matters most, but what people say *under* what people say that matters —and what TRULY matters even more is what people THEN say back, in response, or RATHER what people say under what they are saying IN RESPONSE to what people said under what they said—if you know what I mean.

What I'm getting at *is* actually a serious point. A lot of what goes on in business meetings goes on in "subtitles"—like that very funny scene in *Annie Hall,* where Woody Allen and Diane Keaton are saying one thing, while their private thoughts about making love are flashing on the screen. Only in business:

"Making love" = *kissing up or fucking the*
other over.

As I've mentioned in some prior chapters, often:

I'm sorry = *you'll be sorry.*

or

Your idea is not right for us = *HOWEVER,*
after you leave and we make your idea our very
own, then your idea will be very right for us.

The ability to know the good guys from the bad guys is an invaluable Darwinian business survival skill in a business world that can be a jungle inhabited by two-headed beasts—more commonly known as "The Two-Faced Businessperson." (I suppose having that second face can come in handy for these people. If/when they get caught and lose face, they'll always have another left.)

When a woman listens closely to her intuition, she's told what she should and should not reveal to others in a meeting, enabling her to think fast on her feet. And a woman who's good on her feet will be monetarily rewarded.

Since paying attention to our female intuition can pay off monetarily in the long run, we women must be sure to indulge in more . . .

Power Hunches

AND we women must allow these power hunches to digest fully in our gut—literally. Our gut is physically where we first feel our emotions, hence the expression "gut reaction."

You've experienced strong gut reactions to people, I'm sure. And ignored them, too, at times, I'm sure. An ignored gut reaction is what I mean by a badly digested power hunch—one we don't pay attention to, and one that can lead to real physical gut manifestations, like nausea or even ulcers. These symptoms often occur because your body is taking on the discomfort of your intuitive heart, serving as your being's backup alarm system, hoping to get your attention, since your intuitive heart failed in trying to warn you to slow down and be on guard about the potential dangers of a person or a situation.

SO . . . if from the start of a business transaction you sense a flurry in your stomach, pay attention—BIG TIME. We women must learn not only to read *other* people's body language, but *our own* body language as well, beginning with what our bellies can belie.

I guess it's not so surprising that we don't listen to our gut. This society doesn't really respect/value the invisible/emotional world as much as the visible/rational world, which is a shame because the former often influences our lives in a much bigger way than the latter. Think about it. The invisible/emotional world is where life-altering encounters like love and sexual attraction are played out. If we trust our gut's opinion in these personal realms, we should trust our gut's opinion in business realms as well. After all, people are still people, with the same emotional dynamics, whether across a crowded dance floor or across a crowded conference table.

In the book *Heart Sutra: Ancient Buddhist Wisdom in the Light of Quantum Reality* by Mu Soeng, the author notes:

> *"It is not an accident that the Chinese word*
> *'hsin' stands for 'Heart-Mind.' In the Eastern*
> *way of looking at things, the thinking-feeling*
> *process is a unified field, in contrast to the*
> *Cartesian dualism of the Western*
> *scientific mind."*

Surprisingly, one of our nation's most admired scientific minds was an exception to this rule. Einstein was a fan of intuition. He used it in his research, explaining:

> *"There is no logical way to the discovery of*
> *these elemental laws. There is only the way of*
> *intuition, which is helped by a feeling for the*
> *order lying behind appearance."*

This intuition is the invisible force behind all innovative ideas, as well as the mysterious power that separates a smart chess player from a brilliant one, a good chef from an unbelievable one, and a proficient writer from an inspired one. In other words, intuition is that thing that's called upon when you play chess, cook, or write with an aware and humming heart.

The East more than the West respects these radar powers of the heart to get you where you need to go, recognizing that the heart is just as smart an organ as the brain—if not the smarter at times—and a genius of an organ compared to our eyes, which for the most part are pretty foolish and gullible, believing everything they see. Appearances,

as we know, are often highly deceptive. Which reminds me of a good
Taoist tale . . .

Horse Sense

*There was this King guy who had this mar-
velously talented Horse Picker, who knew how
to pick from a stable full of horses only the
fastest and fiercest. Unfortunately, this Horse
Picker was very ill and was soon to die. The
King asked this Horse Picker if, before he
passed on, he could find a replacement so the
King could continue to have the fastest and
fiercest horses in the kingdom. The Horse
Picker agreed not to die until he had done so,
and a month later he returned to the kingdom
with his replacement. The King asked the Horse
Picker to stay alive a bit longer until he could
test out the replacement's skills at finding winning horses. He agreed. The replacement was
then sent out on a horse hunt and returned a
week later with great news. He'd found a
miraculously fast yellow mare that would be
arriving the next day, UPS. The next day, the
King went to see it, but found instead a black
stallion. The King was incensed by the stupidity
of this replacement, to not know a yellow mare
from a black stallion. He stormed into the
Horse Picker's quarters, hoping he was still
alive so he could threaten his life. The Horse
Picker was, and immediately went to the sta-
bles to see what had happened. There in the*

field he saw, as the King had described, a black
stallion running. The Horse Picker excitedly
returned to the King and said: "King, you are
right about that black stallion. It is, as you
said, black and a stallion. And I am right about
my replacement. He is talented—in fact, even
more talented than I had originally thought. He
is a man who far exceeds my skills at finding
the ultimate horses, for he is a man who does
not bother to notice whether a horse is yellow
or black or a mare or a stallion. When he looks
at a horse, all he can see is fast horse running.
That's all. He sees only to the underneath part,
to fast horse running.*"*

When in a business meeting, we, too, should always try to see to the underneath part, past the colorful words and promises. We should try to sense whether or not a presentation means "fast money running into our hands"—or running out of our hands, for that matter.

THE GOOD BUSINESS NEWS IS . . . Because we females were socialized at a young age to be cognizant of appearances and mis-appearances —learning *which cosmetics* to wear to look prettier, *which clothes* to wear to look thinner, *which bras* to wear to look . . . uh, "riper"— we've been privy to an education in the art of these surface illusions, and therefore are better adept at intuiting the illusory.

If we want to pick up more clues, we should try talking less and listening to our intuitive hearts more—which requires being fully present in the here and now, rather than caught up in thinking about the past or the future. If we pay attention to the here and now, we will pick up all sorts of revealing details that will fall somewhere between intuition and heightened powers of observation, including:

1. Women have an advanced education in what I call "The Language of Clothes," a complicated dialect with an ever-growing list of adjectives. Women speak it as a first language, unlike men, who need a Berlitz guide (a.k.a. *Women's Wear Daily*) to reach our level of Clothes Understanding. Even better than knowing another's astrology sign is knowing her favorite clothing designer. A woman who has access to this info has access to another's soul. Women know: Every fashion statement expresses an emotional statement, revealing a bit about the person's tastes, confidence, education, sexuality, sense of humor—even politics.

2. *What They Don't Teach You in Harvard Business School* advises being particularly attentive during fringe times—for instance, right before and after meetings, while waiting for the elevator, and while standing at the Xerox machine. People are more relaxed during these times and might reveal interesting details, either about themselves or the goings-on at work.

3. Business meals are full of revealing clues if a savvy woman is on her toes. You can find out a lot about a person by how he orders in restaurants, especially Chinese restaurants. Power positions are revealed in varying ordering styles. For instance, does the individual leave the ordering up to everyone else or take control? Is he unwilling to try new things or eager to take culinary chances? Is he open to sharing or territorial about his entrée? It's also helpful to notice whether or not he gobbles down his food more during certain topics of conversation—e.g., when a specific person is mentioned or project is discussed.

4. Pay attention to a person's choice of words. For instance, I know a guy in business who overuses the word *afraid,* which I find very revealing. Even his business answering machine has the message "I'm afraid I can't come to the phone right now."

5. People's breathing habits are also a great clue. Breathing changes when we are nervous. I have a friend who, whenever he's nervous,

always clears his throat. PLUS, if you listen closely, you'll notice people sigh or breathe more deeply when exasperated. So be aware of the breadth of different breaths a client releases in different circumstances. In poker, these idiosyncracies are called "tells," and when they show, they definitely tell.

Some other logical forms of intuition can be found through the process of what men call "overanalyzing" and women call "just plain analyzing." In other words, we women admittedly often search for deep meaning in the superficial. For instance, when I was growing up my girlfriends and I used to believe that you could tell what a person was all about by who her favorite Beatle was. (In the nineties, the same test works, except it's about who your favorite Baldwin brother is.)

PLUS, we women should also keep in mind that intuition is not only triggered by what people say, but by what people *don't* say. For instance, when someone repeatedly avoids giving a response or delays returning a phone call for a long while, we must listen to our power hunches to give us clues about what that means. (Unfortunately, however, in today's time-starved times, it's getting harder and harder to tell the difference between someone who says he's too busy to return a phone call and someone who really *is* too busy to return a phone call. There should almost be some sort of code as to which "busy" you really are. Like a "I'm really busy right now quack-quack." You know, a little something to distinguish the two "I'm busys.")

Although, as I explained earlier, a lot of people-reading skills can be attributed to heightened observation skills and common sense, a lot of intuition could also be about a sixth sense—a sense to which women are especially attuned.

The mystical sciences have always recognized that women are gifted with superior psychic inclinations, which was noticed especially during that witch-hunt period—as well as during one's "period" period. The mystics believe that during her menstrual cycle, a woman is sup-

267

posed to be especially intuitive, which they believe explains why she's moodier: She's twice as sensitive to picking up energy and vibes from the universe. THIS is yet another good reason why women should be given more decision-making positions. We could put our psychic powers to work predicting marketing trends—and even more important, intuiting what is the best dish to order for lunch.

BUT before you consider trading in having balls at a meeting for having crystal balls, consider that . . .

THERE ARE DISADVANTAGES TO THIS FEMALE ADVANTAGE

*T*he same emotional sensory bonanza that endows a woman with intuition also bestows her with more facial expression. This richer inner emotional world eventually makes its appearance in the outer world on a woman's face. A woman's face—more than a man's—tends to show more of everything she's feeling, because there *is* more of everything that a woman is feeling. Contrarily, a man can be harder to read than Sartre in his native French tongue.

A woman therefore can be at a disadvantage at meetings in which a poker face is needed—unless she is mindful of how her face looks at all times.*

Another disadvantage to all this intuition is that a woman who becomes too secure in her intuition could become overly confident of her intuitive abilities, and every once in a while, unbeknownst to herself, misinterpret that . . .

---

*NOTE: Just think of the auxiliary benefit: fewer wrinkles, fewer wrinkles, fewer wrinkles.

*A cigar is not just a cigar, but a submachine
gun aimed at her cranium.*

Paranoia can find a home where wise intuition once resided, and a woman might begin to intuit too big a deal out of a little thing. She could misinterpret another's unfamiliar cultural cues or individual quirks and mistakenly take things personally. *Or* she could read a person right, but misinterpret wrong—e.g., read a person's negativity as a bad reaction to a presentation, when it could just be a bad reaction to lunch. All of which reminds me of an old joke that should be taken very seriously:

Running on Empty Information

*A man's car ran out of gas in the middle of the
boondocks with no gas station in sight. This
need-of-gas guy found an empty gallon cannis-
ter in his trunk and started walking to a mansion he could see in the distance on top of this
high mountain. As this need-of-gas guy was
walking, he thought to himself how he could
imagine getting all the way to that mansion and
having the man who answered the door be
snobby, or not trust him, think he was a thief or
a runaway convict. This need-of-gas guy imagined how he'd have to plead with the mansion
man to trust him, and lend him gas. This need-
of-gas guy imagined how the mansion man
might want to charge him—or overcharge
him—for the favor, and how obnoxious that
would be considering he lived in that big mansion. As this need-of-gas guy walked, he got*

angrier and angrier for the hard time the man-
sion man would give. Finally this need-of-gas
guy got to the mansion door and knocked. When
the mansion man answered, this need-of-gas
guy took one look at him and said, "Well, I
don't want your goddamn gas anyway!" and
stormed away.

So never hold on to your intuitive interpretations too possessively. Wait. Test out your theory first—as subtly as possible. *Then* respond to the situation based on your informed intuition.

Synchronistically, the day I was working on this chapter, I was in my neighborhood where I saw a door that had a little inscription on the bottom: INTUIT. I pointed the inscription out to a friend, who read it out loud with a different emphasis: IN . . . TU . . . IT. As in " I'm into it." Then I noticed the word was even spaced out to be read with this alternate emphasis, reminding me ONCE AGAIN that there's always more than one interpretation for anything, and you should be careful not to give something the wrong emphasis—the familiar emphasis, the *learned* emphasis—as if it is the *only perspective.*

The good news/bad news about life is:

Most of the time another person's bad behavior
has absolutely nothing to do with you.

That's right. Nada. Zilcho. Sorry. Usually it has to do with the other person's own overweight ego, which creates what I euphemistically call "limitations." And it's these "limitations" that often prevent us from see-ing alternate realities, from seeing with the best kind of vision there is: the vision of clarity.

$Staremaster$
For Building Intuition

1. Star watch. A woman should use her intuition to be aware of shooting-star employees who are just little shots now but growing and glowing increasingly brighter and brighter. Get to know them in advance. They'll remember and appreciate your support later.

2. Practice your intuitive skills at your next meeting. Pretend you are watching a movie without sound. (WARNING: Do not do this for more than thirty-second intervals or you could miss something crucial.) The goal is to listen *less* to the exact words people say, and *more* to *how* they're saying them. What does their body language say behind their back? How are they sitting? Are they playing nervously with their pencil when asked about financial explanations? Do both their socks match? Are they wearing sock garter belts?

3. The Time-Life book *The Brain* reveals a good tip about body language: It can be a self-fulfilling prophecy, because not only does information flow from brain to body BUT body to brain. The book recommends fighting a low mood by "put[ting] the cart before the horse." If you smile, stand tall, walk with a spring in your step, and/or generally act in good spirits, your emotions will eventually catch up.

4. If you have a very important business conversation coming up, make sure you have it in person, not on the telephone. You'll gather more clues about their psyches and therefore be at an advantage not only during this conversation but also in future interactions with this person.

5. The corporate world suddenly smells like team spirituality. There's a trend toward trusting our spirit's intuition and actually

caring about the spiritual aspects of our world, by exploring products and services that can enhance our spirituality—all of which tap into a woman's innate spiritual tendencies, meaning opening up the ladies' room door for more opportunities for women.

Part 4

THE RISE

AND FALL

OF THE PENIS

TAKE ME OUT OF
THE BALLS GAMES

Soon after I quit my job in advertising, I took a screenwriting seminar where I was taught the secret of creating multidimensional fictional characters. The professor advised us NOT to show a character going through his day-to-day rituals, or else nothing of substance would be learned. To reveal a character's inner essence, throw him into a conflict and/or force him to undergo major change. THIS, said the professor, is the ONLY way to ever truly show and know who a fictional character is deep down in his beating and bursting fictional heart.

I thought: Same goes for us flesh-and-blood characters.

As a girl who had just traded in her high-paying, secure job in advertising for the ethereal hope of becoming a novelist, I was being introduced to conflict and major change on an intimate level. It was interesting (yes, that's one of those euphemistic "interestings") interacting with new people without my "Hello, My Name Is Karen, I Am an Advertising Senior VP" intro ID tag, and watching how differently others viewed me — *the same me.* Or was I the same me?

I related to how soldiers must feel when they return to civilian life, strip off their uniforms and medals, slip into nonmilitary clothes, and go out into the world. Or more to the point, I related to how recovering amnesia victims must feel, each day discovering new things about one's primal self, each day asking oneself:

Who am I?

As a girl who no longer had an embossed business card to her name
—or with my name—I had to ask myself:

Who am I
when I am
not doing
but
just being?

Sitting there in that writing seminar as a newly indicted ritual-free
individual, I realized just how right that professor was: Day-to-day rituals *do* prevent a character from showing/knowing her inner essence.
AND. . . .

This is why: *Most people avoid change.*

Because: *Most people don't want to show/know*
their inner essence.

This showing/knowing can be frightening. It's been acknowledged:

Ignorance is bliss.

Which also comes with its unacknowledged implication:

Awareness can be blistering.

Each of us has unique strategies to avoid seeing who we are under
our fecund facade. A popular strategy is to develop:

Ms. McGoo Vision

Because of our fear of the inner unknown, many women become
like female Mr. McGoos, viewing the world in a hazy, dreamlike, half-
asleep state. The benefits? Blurry outer vision happily leads to blurry

inner vision. After all, the less info we let inside our heads, the less info we *get* inside our heads to potentially tell us who we really are.

Ms. McGoo vision therefore can be much less threatening than keen, alert vision, which allows us to see life all too clearly—including clearly seeing all those "holes" in the street mentioned in that "Autobiography in Five Chapters" poem (from *The Tibetan Book of Living and Dying,* in Part 2), as well as all those mirrors that circumstances in life hold up to our face in an attempt to show us what's wrong with us and needs to be fixed.

With Ms. McGoo vision we're unable to see these holes or these mirrored reflections of our imperfect self, that unadorned self that exists without our prettified social makeup on, that unadorned self that can be rather disappointing to behold—or even shocking. A Ms. McGoo wisely knows this and that . . .

What we can't see can't depress us.

A Ms. McGoo believes:

Out of sight, out of mind.

What a Ms McGoo, however, does not realize is:

Out of sight can mean out of insight.

Or worse . . .

Out of sight can mean "out of our minds."

We can start to feel depressed or anxious and not know what is causing these feelings. How can we know when our Ms. McGoo vision has prevented us from taking a good clear look at who we are and what we are doing with our lives?

Many Ms. McGoos choose to blame their chemicals instead of the chemistry they've set up with others in business or love—and often at this point turn to Prozac for help. In many ways, Prozac is the richer woman's crack. Both drugs promote the denial of reality—or support what Tom Wolfe once said:

"Reality is a nice place to visit but I wouldn't want to live there."

I believe, however, that if you become a resident of reality, you get some wonderful perks. Sure, reality is not all picnics and Andy Garcia. It has its problems. But for that matter, so does Ms. McGoo vision. The biggie:

It's hard to get to your destination if you aren't aware of where you are or where you're going.

And Ms. McGoo vision is unsafe to boot. After all, a Ms. McGoo, unlike Mr. McGoo, is not lucky enough to be continually protected from unseen obstacles in her path.

Though a Ms. McGoo does have one thing going for her that Mr. McGoo never had: Occasionally she awakens from her somnolent condition.

That's great news, right?

Well, it can be—as long as she resists the urge to press that snooze button and say:

Later. I'll wake up to reality later. Later, later, later.

Basically, most of us can be procrastinators of self-evolvement. Myself included. I've always found it bizarre that I can lead a double life both as "Wait Problem Girl" and "I'll Get Around to That Later Girl."

Usually these "awakenings" occur when a Ms. McGoo sleepwalks into a situation where the honking and shouting is so loud that she has no choice but to realize she has been sleepwalking through her life.

I described this state earlier as a "kriya," and it can come in the form of a serious illness, a pink slip, another woman's slip in your paramour's briefcase—whatever. But there you are, sobbing over a mug of Cappuccino Commotion, realizing:

This is my life and I'll krya if I want to.

In Alcoholics Anonymous a krya is recognized as that moment when one is finally able to say:

I am an alcoholic, and this is no way to live.

For me, as an advertising senior VP, I experienced this moment as:

I am a workaholic and this is no way to live.

I suddenly realized I needed to spend less time doing, more time being. I realized I needed to have more "just be" in my life and less "busy bee." What I'm getting at is . . .

I needed to have more balance *in my life.*

I was feeling exhausted and emotionally depleted due to this overloading of "do."

Unfortunately, I'm not the only one in this country who has experienced these effects from that cause. As often is the case, what's true for the micro is true for the macro.

This country has drifted out of balance, driven by its: do, do, do, get more bananas, get more bananas, get more bananas attitude—and now this country is experiencing a krya from this overwhelming emphasis.

I believe the conflicts and internal societal rumblings we've been reading about in the paper and watching on Court TV are our country's kriyas, forcing us to finally look around and see the detrimental effects this imbalance of "over-doing" has had on our stock market, our economy, our environment, our family structure, our—well, you get where I'm going.

We are now paying our dues for too many of our do, do, dos. Finally we are reexamining our country's unspoken but all-too-lived motto "Do or die," recognizing that too much of the "do" part can lead us into the latter part.

To avoid the potential problems ahead, this country has been instinctively seeking to balance itself out.

How?

By trying to experience more "be." We are seeing this renewed appreciation for "just being" expressed in our renewed appreciation for spirituality, the environment, the family, etc. This country is calling on more of its "be" moments—which are, when it comes down to it:

More of its female energies

After all, "being" is a stereotypical female trait, whereas "doing" is stereotypically male.

I believe what I experienced as an "imbalanced woman" was an imbalance that was favoring my stereotypically male qualities and fighting against my stereotypically female qualities. My internal anima/animus (mentioned in Part 1) were at war with each other—and not just when it came to creating a balance of do versus be, but other male versus female qualities, many of which were mentioned in Part 3, and many more of which are listed below:

Boy Meets Girl Characteristics

masculine	feminine
macho	sweetie-poo-pie
conquer	merge
doing	being
rational	intuitive
strong	vulnerable
mental	emotional
thing oriented	people-oriented
external explorer	internal explorer

more into the "touch" world	more into the "feelie" world
penis	boobs
hunt	gather
deluxe bacon-cheeseburgers	light salads (followed by pig-outs on chocolate)
needs to know answers	wants to ask questions
single-minded	multiminded
sees destinations	sees journey
transaction-oriented	relationship-oriented
sees in terms of *a* to *b* to *c*	sees how *a* relates to *c*, how *b* relates to *f*, and how *b* and *d* might relate
sexually oriented	romantically oriented

As an advertisingaholic, I was having trouble not only dealing with that balance of doing versus being, but that balance between being aggressive or being a sweetie-pie-poo, or being rational versus being intuitive. In fact, just go down the above list and you'll have a list of the internal war I was fighting within myself.

Part of me was ashamed of calling upon my female side at the office, or out of the office, for that matter. I was experiencing internally my own "Anima/Animus/Enemies" problem that I mentioned in Part 1 —the same one society was/is engaging in externally all around me, with Amazon Girls as a growing group.

Once again, what I experienced was merely a micro result of the macro problem of this country.

I believe America as a country has been fighting against its stereo-typically female qualities, and has been a bit ashamed of them, afraid it will be thought of as wimpy for showing its female side, and thereby has been overcompensating by putting too much emphasis on its male qualities.

Just look at America compared to the countries of the East and you will see just how stereotypically male we have been acting. If America were to be personified, it would definitely be a guy person. And a real "guy-guy," who was always running around, talking loudly, smacking you on the back in greeting, and occasionally belching. A lovable, rambunctious guy-guy.

Now imagine a country, say, like India, personified as a person. It would be female: silent, still, spiritual.

And America would have a hard time understanding it—in the same way many a man has a hard time understanding many a woman.

Because what we know feels safe . . . and right . . . and better.

However, neither of us—be we man or woman, America or India—are right or wrong.

What we are wrong about is not accepting that we need to have a balance of both our male and female energies. Because when we do, this balance creates harmony.

When we deny the existence and even the benefits of either our male side or our female side, we only exhaust our spirit, because each side is after all the shadow side of the other. As the Taoists say:

> *When you pick up one end of the stick,*
> *the other end comes up with it.*

Any attempts to fight against our male or female side are as energy wasting and futile as a cat chasing after its own shadow on a wall. Instead, each of us—both men and women—needs to stop thinking about picking either/or when it comes to things like doing versus being or being aggressive versus being sweetie-poo-pie or any and all of the male/female characteristics I listed earlier.

Instead we must *learn to develop and accept* our opposite modes—which I guess is what *this whole book is about.*

We must learn to unite rather than fight our dualities.

The result won't be androgyny as we've known it, but synergy as we've yet to know it.

Our power will rise
(both as a country and as individuals).
And Prozac sales will decline.

Two Specific Examples to Help Clear Away Any Remaining Ms. McGoo Vision as to What the Heck This Book Is About:

1. Let's say you're the type of person who's instinctively aggressive at the office. You should try laying low for a bit, save up your energies, let things come toward you, instead of going full force toward them.

or

2. Let's say you're the type of country that's instinctively aggressive about everything. We as a country should try laying low for a bit, save up our energies, let things come toward us, instead of going full force toward them.

Both we as individuals and we as a country must learn to be proud of being both tough and tender—à la Perdue—and learn to appreciate both our darker areas and lighter areas, à la Perdue.

We must stop polarizing ourselves as "that's sooo female" or "that's soooo male," and try instead to be full, complete, balanced humans.

IN OTHER WORDS . . .

To be oneself means to be One Self.

As I mentioned, I believe we are starting to see this shift toward our female energies being displayed in our renewed interest in spirituality, the environment, family values, etc. And because of this, I feel it's easier than ever to answer that Big Question many folks have had about allowing us women into the work force.

That Big Question Being

So, what's in it for me?

The Big Answer Being

*You know those ten female qualities I listed in
Part 3? Well, now more than ever the corporate
world needs these female energies so we as a
country will have more energy and spirit to
pull ourselves up by our bootstraps and get out
of the mess that too much doing, doing, doing
has gotten us into.*

And as Sun Tzu has said:

*"They who can establish a moral cause be-
tween the government and the people will win."*

Well, we women have got the moral cause on our side. The economy needs our female energies, and the family infrastructure needs our
female energies for *balance, balance, balance!*

Actually, when you think about it, a 100 percent all-male environment is not the natural way of this world. This world was created to have
a balance of male/female energies. It makes sense that this rule of nature
logically would apply in the corporate world as well.

It's the way of nature, baby. It's the law.

IT'S A CAT-EAT-CAT WORLD

I don't mean to ruin the celebration of how our female energy is
finally being appreciated, but at the same time, I want to make sure all
of us women are all on the party list of this celebration—that no woman

is left off. And sometimes I worry about how some women treat some women in business. I worry it's not the penises but the vaginas we have to look out for.

Michelle Pfeiffer in *Batman Returns* described the women-in-business situation very well when she said:

"Meow, meow."

Michelle Pfeiffer was right. Unfortunately, all too often the female business world can be a cat race, with all too many women being catty to one another rather than supportive.

Divide and conquer, the expression goes—and so often goes the community of women. Divided it's hard for us to stand. Feminism is divided up so much, it's even been jokingly referred to as "feminisms."

All of this means we're missing out on a valuable opportunity for Girl Networking, enabling us women to get our collective Ferragamoed feet into the door.

According to feminist writer Marilyn French, even female leaders like Golda Meir, Margaret Thatcher, Indira Ghandhi, and Benazir Bhutto once in power did not use their power to truly ease women's lot. With few exceptions, only male leaders dare to eliminate laws constricting women.

When I was in advertising, I experienced a lot of disappointment about how some of the women in charge treated us women coming in. When I was made a senior VP, rather than congratulate me, one woman at the agency actually said:

"You don't know what it is to suffer. You've got-ten everything handed to you so easily. And you know what else I resent about you? You com-plain about being fat, and you're thin."

The funny thing is, when this woman left my office I was in good spirits because I realized that if she was so obviously not my pal yet had

told me I was thin, perhaps it could be true. Perhaps I could be thin.
But I digress.

My point is, a lot of women in business are not helping one another
as much as they could be . . . and for a few reasons:

Cat-Eat-Cat Food for Thought

1. A woman's insecurity about maintaining her own powers—some
   women fear that these powers will disappear at any moment, so they
   think that they shouldn't show any weakness by calling in favors
   from others to help others, because it could dissipate their power.
2. Jealousy could be at play at work—and jealousy is really just another
   word for "bad competition skills." Men, who know from sports how
   to channel their jealousy into inspiration, are better at dealing with
   another's success at the office. It drives them to work harder rather
   than waste their time stewing about the other person's success.
3. A little bit of self-loathing—sometimes not wanting to help others
   (women) who are like ourselves (women) comes from not liking ourselves (women). Plus, you know how abused children often go on to
   abuse their children? Psychologists explain this as learned behavior
   merged with an effort to rationalize and understand one's abuser and
   defend his actions so as to feel less bad about being abused.
   Similarly, a woman might instinctively befriend men in business
   while not supporting businesswomen.
4. Lack of abundance mentality—some women just cannot believe
   there's enough power and jobs to go around to everyone.

CAT TRAINING

$\mathcal{I}$f a woman has done something catty, try not to keep the cat fight going. It becomes like that thread on the hem of your dress that you try to pull off and suddenly the whole hem unravels. Snip the thread of a connection with this woman if possible, but don't keep pulling. Try out this strategy: Befriend thy enemy. As Machiavelli explained:

> "A prince who has a well-fortified city and does not make himself hated cannot be attacked."

Sun Tzu also supported this philosophy when he said:

> "Use your brain to beat the enemy. . . . An able military commander can get the enemy to surrender without fighting."

Of course if possible, it's best to totally avoid a woman who has a reputation for getting into cat fights. If this is her pattern, chances are, if you come into her path, she will get her catty peanut butter on your chocolate destiny—so to speak. And a cat fight can be energy draining, as Sun Tzu explained:

> "Once the war drags on, the troops become tired and their morale suffers."

If you can't physically stay clear of a Cat Woman, at least stay clear mentally, by not spending too much mental energy thinking about her. Once you do start worrying about her, you are giving her the power over you she wants. Plus, again, you are depleting your energy reserves— and time reserves. Remember: Emotional reactions can be distractions from your Career Waldo.

AND . . . as I also mentioned earlier, distrust can be contagious.

When you expect the worst from people, you start to only see the worst. Which reminds me of a story.

Computer Hating

I got a computer at one of the ad agencies where I worked and was given a choice: wait for a computer specialist to put it togther or do it myself. I chose to do it myself. My art director, Kate, was in my office at the time. We both laughed at the dangers and inanity of ME attempting such a thing. Finally, I was ready to flip the switch and see what happened. I did. Seconds later, both Kate and I saw smoke and smelled smoke coming from the direction of the computer. We quickly moved away from it. "Oh my God!" said Kate, dragging on her cigarette. "Did you see that smoke?" she asked, dragging on her cigarette. Then we both realized where the smoke was coming from—and it wasn't my computer. It was from Kate dragging on her cigarette. Because we both expected the worst from me and my computer-assembly skills, we both projected the worst interpretation of the innocent smoke in the air.

So we must watch out for ricocheting distrustful projections. They could land on an innocent woman.

Also, while you're on guard duty, if you've just survived a bad cat fight, keep a watchful eye out for the tendency to overreact to a Cat Woman's minor scratching at you.

So if you've heard rumors that a woman has the potential to be catty, be sure not to overreact to a minor comment she might utter at

288

you. All that might be needed is a cup of coffee with this woman to talk things over.

In cat-eat-cat situations it's always best to respond by striving to understand where the other person is coming from, rather than reacting with anger at this person. The Buddhist writer Shantideva had a good philosophy about all this. He said:

> *foes are as unlimited as [the extent of] space;*
> *they cannot possibly all be overcome.*
> *Yet if you just overcome*
> *the thought of hatred*
> *that will be equal to overcoming all foes*
> *where is the leather*
> *with which one can cover the earth?*
> *But wearing a leather sandal*
> *Is equal to covering the earth with leather*

What you give to others emotionally will be what you receive back. So give kindness and understanding to other women as much as possible. And be sure to be as equally kind to the assistants you deal with as the muckee-mucks. As Machiavelli explained:

> *"Conciliate to the people rather than the sol-*
> *diers because the people are the more*
> *powerful."*

People who answer phones for muckee-mucks are some of the most powerful people in the world. First, of course, because these people have their boss's ear. Second because these people could very well grow up to be muckee-mucks themselves.

My last bit of advice for helping other women in business: Be sure to set up a reputation for yourself that you are there to give advice and assistance to other women—then live up to this reputation. And if you're too busy to help someone, there's a simple solution. Just let them know that there's this really amazing book they can turn to for help called *How to Succeed in Business Without a Penis*. In fact, do your Girl Networking duty, and start a *How to Succeed in Business Without a Penis* book chain letter, where you must send ten of these books to ten new people on a list, and so on and so on and so on.

(Just kidding, just kidding! Hey, you can take the girl out of the advertising agency, but you can't take the advertising agency out of the girl, you know?)

Anyway, in the spirit of Girl Networking, I've gathered some advice from women who prefer it on top, in this next section:

A CHICK LIST

1. Madonna, singer/human tornado: "I'm tough, ambitious, and I know exactly what I want. If that makes me a bitch, okay."
2. Oprah Winfrey, talk-show host: "Power was never a goal. You should stand for excellence and what will happen will happen."
3. Judy McGrath, president of MTV: "I think you have to have a point of view, show up every day, be dependable, do the job, have a passion and be relentless about it."
4. Jamie McDermott, executive producer of *Friends* and TV producer success story extraordinaire: "I've been lucky enough to always work for people who have given me a lot of respect. . . . Also, I believe as they say, the play's the thing. It's not about the politics and who you know."
5. Pauline R. Kezer, Connecticut Secretary of State: "The glass ceiling gets more pliable when you turn up the heat!"
6. Roseanne, comedienne (from that *New Yorker* interview): "People say to me, 'You're not very feminine.' Well, they can just *suck my dick.*"
7. Barbara Walters, TV interviewer: "Trust your gut."

8. Erma Bombeck, humorist: "When I stand before God at the end of my life, I would hope that I would not have a single bit of talent left and could say: 'I used everything you gave me.'"

9. Fay Weldon, writer: "Worry less about what other people think of you, and more about what you think about them."

10. Cher, singer/actress: "If you really want something, you can figure out how to make it happen."

11. Diane Arbus, photographer: "My favorite thing is to go where I've never been."

12. Gail Sheehy, psychologist/sociologist: "If we don't change, we don't grow. If we don't grow, we are not really living."

13. Billie Jean King, tennis champion: "Be bold. If you're going to make an error make a doozy, and don't be afraid to hit the ball."

14. Katharine Hepburn, actress: "As for me, prizes mean nothing. My prize is my work."

15. Beverly Sills, opera singer: "You may be disappointed if you fail, but you are doomed if you don't try."

16. Helen Hayes, actress: "If you rest, you rust."

17. Margaret Thatcher, former British prime minister: "One only gets to the top rung on the ladder by steadily climbing up one at a time, and suddenly all sorts of powers, all sorts of abilities . . . become within our own possibility and you think, 'Well, I'll have a go, too.'"

18. Rosalynn Carter, former First Lady: "I had already learned from more than a decade of political life that I was going to be criticized no matter what I did, so I might as well be criticized for something I wanted to do. (If I had spent all day 'pouring tea,' I would have been criticized for that too.)"

19. Tallulah Bankhead, actress: "If I had to do it over again, I'd make the same mistakes, only sooner."

20. Bella Abzug, U.S. Congresswoman: "Our struggle today is not

to have a female Einstein get appointed as an assistant professor. It is for a woman schlemiel to get as quickly promoted as a male schlemiel."

21. Twyla Tharp, choreographer: "Eventually, I realized that I didn't have to 'become' a man to be powerful."

22. Sojourner Truth, spiritual guide: "If the first woman God ever made was strong enough to turn the world upside down all alone, these women together ought to be able to turn it back, and get it right side up again! And now they is asking to do it, and men better let them."

23. Grace Mirabella, editor: "Determined, fearless women are redefining glamour. It's their unremitting talent and smarts that make the difference now."

24. Charlotte Whitton, Mayor of Ottawa: "Whatever women do they must do twice as well as men to be thought half as good. Luckily, this is not difficult."

25. Ann Watt, president of Ann Watt PR: "Do charity work related to your work. Take on more than you think you can handle, but be responsible. Take time to know you are a mentor to young people because you can absolutely change someone else's life. Pass on résumés from young people to others. Think of yourself as an employment opportunity."

26. Gloria Salmansohn, actress/author's mom: "I once heard an expression that has stayed with me: 'If you do what you've always done, you'll get what you always get.' "

27. Leesil Schillenger, writer/researcher at *The New Yorker* magazine: "Get as much stuff done on the phone with people you haven't met. Particularly men. Particularly if you have a good sexy voice. Because when a man finally meets the living breathing you, he will always be thinking: 'Is this someone who would've turned me down in high school?' It's no accident that my career took off with unknown editors I met over the

phone—because I made my voice purr."

28. Sydney Biddle Barrows, writer/entrepreneur of sorts: "No matter how desperate you are, don't sell out or it will come back to haunt you. Self-esteem pays off. Also, be sure to help others. If everybody gives, everybody gets."

29. Julie Just, senior editor, *New York* magazine: "Any potential enemy you have in the office, you should make peace with. Befriend."

30. Charette Boegarte, painter: "I always pay attention to the details. I don't just mean in my painting, but in all things. Appreciation for details takes a certain concentration, and when you got it . . . well, it all seems to come together."

31. August Gold, minister: "Slow down and listen to your intuition. Meditate at least twice a day. Once in the morning, once at night. Muslims have devoted themselves to this practice five times a day. Finding the time to do it twice a day should not be so difficult."

32. Rosalie Osias, real estate lawyer: "What starts off as flirting turns into business. . . . The way I see it, my brain doesn't function differently if I'm wearing a miniskirt or a conservative suit. I'm Rosalie Osias, and I'm a great lawyer and I dress the way I dress. . . . "

33. Judith Newman, writer: "Be loyal to the people that are good to you."

34. Anonymous book agent: "Flattery works."

A LAST-MINUTE WARNING

As you go toward your goal, things might start to look worse before they look better. But this will be a good sign. It will mean you really are changing and that you are experiencing better clarity of your life. Which reminds me of

Some More Bazooka Joe Zen Wisdom

A painter is talking to Bazooka Joe as he paints. He says, "You know, Joe, I paint and I paint and I paint, and not only isn't my painting getting any better, it's getting worse."

And Bazooka Joe responds: "It's not that your painting is getting worse, it's that your taste is getting better."

You will expereince a form of this on your path to change. As you gain more clarity, you will see what's sorta kinda wrong about how you've been living thus far, and things will look worse for a while before they look better. But trust me. This is good. It's sort of like when you go for a facial and your skin gets red and blotchy, but you know your skin will be better for it in the long run. I hope you will be able to see with this long-term vision.

If I had one goal for this book—my Book Waldo—it would be to impart upon you the importance of finding clarity in your life. In fact, I believe if you ever stumble upon a magic bottle that when rubbed will give you one wish and one wish only, the wish you should request is:

May I gain more clarity.

If you ask for this one wish, you'll get all your other wishes FREE! After all, with improved clarity you will be able to see through the blurry wall of your Ms. McGoo vision, past the smudges of your emotions—fear, anger, jealousy, impatience, sadness, loneliness, hatred, self-hatred, hunger for more Snackwell cookies. And it's all of these emotions that are stopping you from seeing clearly what needs to be done to reach your goal. HOWEVER . . . with improved clarity you will truly know what activities are time wasters, what people are energy drainers. With improved clarity you will truly know if you should quit a job or take a job. With improved clarity you will truly know how to separate pleasing the ego from pleasing your highest, truest self. With improved clarity you will truly know how to create the right balance of your male and female energies. With improved clarity you will truly know how to make all the right choices in life. And most important, you will see that you do have choices in life. Some people never, ever get to see this at all.

I believe making the decision to select those choices that make you most happy is a once-in-a-lifetime opportunity. And an opportunity that can begin . . . starting . . .

NOW. Okay . . . Go!!

No, wait. Wait, wait, wait. I forgot something. I have, as so many of us do . . .

One Last Thing

I knew I must be a competitive person when I went to my ten-year high-school reunion and found, to my own embarrassment, that one thought flowed boldly and brightly through my head as I looked around the room:

    Okay. Who won?

    I was not proud of this reaction. But there it was.

Then I wondered:

Okay. What is winning?

Lynn is a doctor. Sarah is a schoolteacher. Is one more of a winner than another? Phoebe is the mother of three children and doesn't work. Is she more or less of a winner than Beth, who works in PR but is single? What is winning?

Then I looked at Marcy. Marcy was a lawyer and married to another lawyer. But Marcy was not a winner. I don't know why I thought it— and knew it—but I just did. Why, I wondered, was Marcy not a winner when by society's standards she had won?

Then it hit me. Marcy's spirit had been broken. You could tell just by looking at her.

And that's when I realized what "winning" is for women today. It's about remaining a full-service feeling, reacting, sexy, sensual woman, not just a career-oriented machine. It's about achieving your goals without letting your balls get busted—and without letting your boobs get busted, either.

The End . . .

or

The Beginning . . .

depending upon your perspective.

Index

Garcia, Andy, 40, 42, 45, 106, 110, 204, 231, 232, 278

paramour, 32, 129, 145, 279
penis, 1, 2, 3, 4, 5 . . . you get the idea
prolixity, 74

SnackWell's cookies, xv